21ST CENTURY COMMUNICATION

LISTENING, SPEAKING, AND CRITICAL THINKING

3

LYNN BONESTEEL

NATIONAL GEOGRAPHIC LEARNING | CENGAGE Learning

Australia • Brazil • Mexico • Singapore • United Kingdom • United States

21st Century Communication: Listening,
Speaking, and Critical Thinking
Student Book 3
Lynn Bonesteel

Publisher: Sherrise Roehr

Executive Editor: Laura Le Dréan

Managing Editor: Jennifer Monaghan

Senior Development Editor: Mary Whittemore

Associate Development Editor: Lisl Trowbridge

Media Research: Leila Hishmeh

Director of Global and U.S. Marketing: Ian Martin

Product Marketing Manager: Anders Bylund

Sr. Director, Production: Michael Burggren

Manager, Production: Daisy Sosa

Content Project Manager: Mark Rzeszutek

Senior Digital Product Manager: Scott Rule

Manufacturing Planner: Mary Beth Hennebury

Interior Design: Brenda Carmichael

Compositor: SPi Global

For product information and technology assistance, contact us at
Cengage Learning Customer & Sales Support, cengage.com/contact

For permission to use material from this text or product,
submit all requests online at **cengage.com/permissions**
Further permissions questions can be emailed to
permissionrequest@cengage.com

Student Book:
ISBN: 978-1-305-95546-2

Student Book with Online Workbook Sticker Code:
ISBN: 978-1-337-27582-8

National Geographic Learning
20 Channel Center Street
Boston, MA 02210
USA

National Geographic Learning, a Cengage Learning Company, has a mission to bring the world to the classroom and the classroom to life. With our English language programs, students learn about their world by experiencing it. Through our partnerships with National Geographic and TED, they develop the language and skills they need to be successful global citizens and leaders.

Locate your local office at **international.cengage.com/region**

Visit National Geographic Learning online at **NGL.cengage.com**
Visit our corporate website at **www.cengage.com**

Printed in China
Print Number: 07   Print Year: 2021

Reviewers

The authors and publisher would like to thank the following teachers from all over the world for their valuable input during the development process of the 21st Century Communication series.

Coleeta P. Abdullah, *EducationKSA, Saudi Arabia*

Ghada Al Attar, *AMIDEAST, Yemen*

Yazeed Al Jeddawy, *AMIDEAST, United Kingdom*

Zubidah Al Sallami, *AMIDEAST, Netherlands*

Ammar Al-Hawi, *AMIDEAST, Yemen*

William Albertson, *Drexel University English Language Center, Pennsylvania*

Tara Arntsen, *Northern State University, South Dakota*

Kevin Ballou, *Kobe College, Japan*

Nafisa Bintayeh, *AMIDEAST, Yemen*

Linda Bolet, *Houston Community College, Texas*

Tony Carnerie, *UCSD Extension, English Language Institute, California*

Catherine Cheetham, *Tokai University, Japan*

Celeste Coleman, *CSUSM American Language and Culture Institute, California*

Amy Cook, *Bowling Green State University, Ohio*

Katie Cottier, *University of Texas at Austin, Texas*

Teresita Curbelo, *Instituto Cultural Anglo Uruguayo, Uruguay*

Sarah de Pina, *ELS Boston Downtown, Massachusetts*

Rachel DeSanto, *Hillsborough Community College, Florida*

Silvana Dushku, *Intensive English Institute, Illinois*

Jennie Farnell, *University of Bridgeport, Connecticut*

Rachel Fernandez, *UCI Extension, International Programs, California*

Alayne Flores, *UCSD Extension, English Language Institute, California*

Claire Gimble, *Virginia International University, Virginia*

Floyd H. Graham III, *Kansai Gaidai University, Japan*

Kuei-ping Hsu, *National Tsing Hua University*

James Hughes, *Massachusetts International Academy / UMass Boston, Massachusetts*

Mariano Ignacio, *Centro Universitario de Idiomas, Argentina*

Jules L. Janse van Rensburg, *Chinese Culture University, South Africa*

Rachel Kadish, *GEOS Languages Plus Boston, Massachusetts*

Anthony Lavigne, *Kansai Gaidai University, Japan*

Ai-ping Liu, *National Central University Language Center*

Debra Liu, *City College of San Francisco, California*

Wilder Yesid Escobar Almeciga Imeciga, *Universidad El Bosque, Colombia*

Christina Lorimer, *SDSU American Language Institute, California*

Joanna Luper, *Liberty University, Virginia*

Joy MacFarland, *FLS Boston Commons, Massachusetts*

Elizabeth Mariscal, *UCSD Extension, English Language Institute, California*

Susan McAlister, *Language & Culture Center, University of Houston, Texas*

Wendy McBride, *Spring International Language Center at the University of Arkansas, Arkansas*

Monica McCrory, *University of Texas, Texas*

Katherine Murphy, *Massachusetts International Academy, Massachusetts*

Emily Naber, *Washington English Center, Washington*

Kavitha Nambisan, *University of Tennessee-Martin, Tennessee*

Sandra Navarro, *Glendale Community College, California*

Fernanda Ortiz, *Center for English as a Second Language at the University of Arizona, Arizona*

Pamela Patterson, *Seminole State College, Oklahoma*

Grace Pimcias, *CSUSM American Language and Culture Institute, California*

Jennie Popp, *Universidad Andres Bello, Chile*

Jamie Reinstein, *Community College of Philadelphia, Pennsylvania*

Philip Rice, *University of Delaware, Delaware*

Helen Roland, *Miami Dade College, Florida*

Yoko Sakurai, *Aichi University, Japan*

Jenay Seymour, *Hongik University (Sejong Campus), South Korea*

Margaret Shippey, *Miami Dade College, Florida*

William Slade, *University of Texas at Austin, Texas*

Kelly Smith, *UCSD Extension, English Language Institute, California*

Rachel Stokes, *University of Texas at Austin, Texas*

Joshua Stone, *Approach International Student Center, Massachusetts*

Judy Tanka, *UCLA Extension, California*

Mary M. Wang, *University of Wisconsin-Madison, Wisconsin*

Judy Wong, *Pace University, New York*

Special thanks to Mary Kadera at TED.

Scope and Sequence

PRONUNCIATION SKILL	NOTE-TAKING SKILL	TED TALKS	PRESENTATION SKILL	UNIT ASSIGNMENT
Intonation and pauses: continuing and concluding	Use abbreviations	*5 ways to kill your dreams* **Bel Pesce**	Pause effectively	Give an individual presentation on "How NOT to learn a foreign language"
Compound words	Focus on main points	*Go ahead, make up new words* **Erin McKean**	Encourage audience participation	Give a pair presentation to teach new words
Syllable stress	Include only essential details	*These robots come to the rescue after a disaster* **Robin Murphy**	Use body language effectively	Participate in a group roleplay about robot designs
Pronouncing –ed endings	Write key words and phrases	*Embrace the shake* **Phil Hansen**	Use repetition and rephrasing	Give an individual presentation about someone who overcame a limitation or used it in order to become successful in some way
Thought groups	Use symbols	*How to make stress your friend* **Kelly McGonigal**	Vary your pace	Conduct a survey on stress and give a group presentation to report the results
Intonation in questions	Rewrite your notes in outline form	*An underwater art museum, teeming with life* **Jason deCaires Taylor**	Be an active participant in a discussion	Participate in and evaluate a group discussion
Stress key words	Use a T-chart to take notes	*Build a school in the cloud* **Sugata Mitra**	Show enthusiasm for your topic	Participate in a panel discussion about Sugata Mitra's School in the Cloud
Intonation in lists	Record information from lists	*Open-sourced blueprints for civilization* **Marcin Jakubowski**	Organize information in a logical sequence	Present and explain a process

Welcome to 21st Century Communication

21st Century Communication: Listening, Speaking, and Critical Thinking develops essential listening, speaking, and presentation skills to help learners succeed with their academic and professional goals. Students learn key academic skills as they engage with thought-provoking TED Talks and 21st century themes and skills, such as global awareness, information literacy, and critical thinking.

Each unit opens with an impactful photograph related to a **21st century theme** and Think and Discuss questions to draw students into the topic.

Part 1 introduces a variety of **listening inputs** including lectures, interviews, podcasts, and classroom discussions.

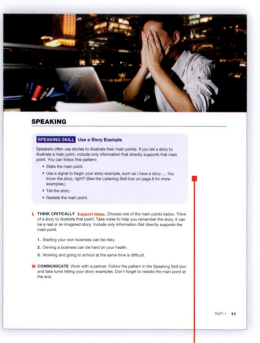

Listening, speaking, note-taking, and pronunciation skills are explicitly taught and practiced. Woven throughout are 21st century skills of **collaboration, communication,** and **critical thinking.**

Part 2 introduces the TED speaker and the idea
worth spreading. Students explore and discuss
the ideas while at the same time seamlessly
applying the skills learned in Part 1.

Infographics engage students more
deeply with the unit theme and promote
visual literacy.

Presentation Skills
inspired by the TED
speakers give students
the skills and authentic
language they need
to successfully
deliver their own
presentations.

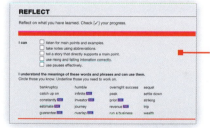

Put It Together helps students **connect
ideas** and prepares them for their final
assignment. Students use a graphic
organizer to synthesize information and
consolidate their learning.

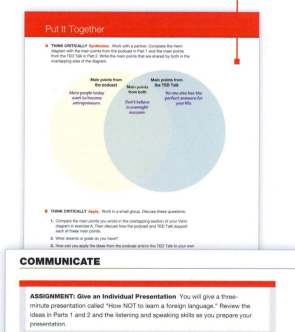

Reflect encourages
students to **take
charge of their
learning**, another
21st century skill.

Fully blended **Online Workbooks powered by
MyELT** help develop **digital literacy skills** by
offering students the complete audio and video
program along with speech-recognition and auto-
graded language practice activities.

Bringing Dreams to Life

Entrepreneur Danielle Baskin owns six businesses. One of her companies is called Inkwell Helmets, which provides hand-painted bicycle helmets. She is ready to invent folding bikes for her next big business idea.

THINK AND DISCUSS

1 Read the unit title. What do you think the title means?

2 Look at the photo and read the caption. How do you think Danielle Baskin's story relates to the unit title?

PART 1 Would-Be-Entrepreneurs: Listen Up!!!

BEFORE YOU LISTEN

A COMMUNICATE Work in a small group. Discuss these questions.

1. Look at the photo and read the caption. What type of business is this? Do you think the products are cheap or expensive? Why?

2. What are some examples of small businesses? What qualities do you think a small business owner should have?

3. Would you like to own your own business? Why, or why not?

B 🎧 **1.2 THINK CRITICALLY Predict.** An entrepreneur is a person who starts a business with an idea, makes it grow, and takes the risk of failure. Listen to the first part of a podcast, *Would-Be-Entrepreneurs: Listen Up!!!* for a program called *Business Talk*. While you are listening, think about the meaning of the title of the podcast. Then with your group, discuss what advice you think the podcaster is going to give his listeners.

Owner Serina Pararajasingam opens Uptown Brie, a new food shop in Toronto, Canada.

VOCABULARY

C 🎧 **1.3** Read and listen to the sentences with words and phrases from the podcast. Guess the meaning of each bold word or phrase. Then write each word or phrase next to its definition.

a. His business success brought him great **wealth** at an early age. He was a billionaire by the age of 30.

b. Experts **estimate** that the number of people employed by small businesses will grow by 10 percent in the next 20 years.

c. Wow, the new design makes the restaurant look completely different. The change is really **striking**.

d. In my country, many young people **settle down** very soon after college. By the age of 30, most are married and have one or two children.

e. That singer was an **overnight success**. One day she was singing in a small club for almost no money, and the next day she had a number-one song.

f. He didn't have any money of his own, so he had to find an **investor** to help him start his business.

g. He has been working 24 hours a day for three days, without any sleep at all. He plans on spending the whole weekend in bed to **catch up on** his sleep.

h. He's retired now. His daughter **runs the business**.

i. She complains **constantly**. She never has anything positive to say.

j. Owning a business is more difficult than most people think. In fact, many small businesses enter into **bankruptcy** within a year or two of opening.

1. _____catch up on_____ (phrasal v) to do something to get back on schedule after falling behind

2. _____constantly_____ (adv) happening all the time, continuously

3. _____settle down_____ (phrasal v) locate and establish (oneself, one's family)

4. _____wealth_____ (n) a large amount of money and property

5. _____investor_____ (n) a person who puts money into a business idea or activity in the hopes of making more money if the idea is successful

6. _____runs the business_____ (v phrase) manages or controls a company or business

7. _____overnight success_____ (n phrase) someone or something that becomes very successful in a very short period of time

8. _____striking_____ (adj) immediately noticeable, usually in a positive or good sense

9. _____estimate_____ (v) figure the approximate (not exact) amount or extent of

10. _____bankruptcy_____ (n) the legal state of being without money

D COMMUNICATE Work with a partner. Read and answer the questions. Use the words and phrases in **bold** in your answers.

> A: *I don't think people with great* **wealth** *are any happier than ordinary people. In fact, I think they are less happy, because they probably always want more* **wealth.** *That's just human nature.*
>
> B: *OK, but I'd rather have* **wealth** *and be unhappy than have nothing and be unhappy!*

1. Are people with great **wealth** happier than ordinary middle class people? Why, or why not?

2. What do you think many entrepreneurs worry about **constantly**?

3. Would you be good at **running a business**? Why, or why not?

4. If you had a million dollars to **invest**, what type of business would you **invest** in? Why?

5. What do you think is the best age for people to **settle down**, get married, and start families? Why?

6. What sometimes happens to people who become **overnight successes**?

LISTEN

learnmore Because it may take some young people in the United States a while to find a job, many college graduates return home to live with their parents after college. This is quite different from the situation in previous decades, when most university graduates would quickly find jobs and set up their own households after graduation.

Rachel Unger, a college graduate, in her room at her parents' house in Montclair, New Jersey, USA

E 🎧 **1.4** ▶ **1.1 LISTEN FOR MAIN IDEAS** Read the statements. Then listen to the podcast and write T for *true* or F for *false* for each statement.

1. ___T___ More young people today want to start their own businesses than in the past.

2. ___F___ The speaker advises young people to get jobs and settle down.

3. ___T___ Many people who want to start their own businesses are not realistic about their chances of success.

4. ___T___ The speaker does not think that most young people are qualified to become entrepreneurs.

WORDS IN THE PODCAST
20 hours straight: 20 hours without stopping or taking a break

F 🎧 **1.5** **LISTEN FOR DETAILS** Listen to each segment of the podcast. Fill in the missing information.

Segment 1

1. Mark Zuckerberg started _face book_ when he was _24_ years old. Today his wealth is estimated at approximately _42_ dollars.

2. Nowadays, many people want to start businesses because of the _Different_ job market and _rapid_ technological change.

3. *Shark Tank* is a _TV_ show on which entrepreneurs try to sell their ideas to _innovator_.

4. Another reason so many people today want to become entrepreneurs is because of the success of people like Mark Zuckerberg and _Bill gates_.

Segment 2

5. Robert owns _a cake_. He works _7_ days a week.

6. He says that small business owners don't have any _free time_.

Segment 3

7. About _one thirded_ of small business owners lose their businesses in the first year and about _one half_ fail within five years.

8. Gail Horvath and her husband ran a successful business for _several_ _30_ _company_ years before the business went into _bankrupcy_. _pasny owner_

Segment 4

9. It can be difficult to have a happy _family / marriag_ when you run your own business.

10. Tony and his wife ended up getting _divorced_ because he _chose_ his business over his wife.

LISTENING SKILL Identify Main Points and Story Examples

When you listen, it's important to identify the speaker's main points and examples. Some examples are short, just a phrase or sentence. Other examples are stories, which can be several sentences long. Read and listen to the example.

🎧 **1.6**

First, running a business is hard work. Just ask Robert. Robert is a French chef who owns a café serving breakfast and lunch . . .

Here are some common expressions that signal story examples:

Just ask (Robert).   *Take (Robert), for example.*

You know the story, right?   *I have a story . . .*

Because this type of example can be long, speakers often restate the main point after the example. Read and listen to how the speaker restates the main point.

*His advice to would-be small business owners? Do not fool yourself. **The freedom of being your own boss might sound great, but say goodbye to free time.***

G 🎧 **1.7** Listen to an excerpt from the podcast. What are the main points? Write them in your own words.

Main point #1: It is very hard work to have your own business.

Main point #2: _____

Main point #3: _____

NOTE-TAKING SKILL Use Abbreviations

To save time when taking notes, use abbreviated forms of key words. One way of abbreviating words is to shorten them by getting rid of a part of the word, or by eliminating some of the vowels *(a, e, i, o, u)*.

NOTE: The examples below are just suggested abbreviations. As you practice taking notes, you will come up with your own abbreviations. The point is to take notes quickly and be able to understand them later.

French ⇒ Fr   breakfast ⇒ brkfst   lunch ⇒ lnch

H 🎧 **1.7** **LISTEN AND TAKE NOTES** Listen again and complete the notes with information from the story examples. Use abbreviations.

	Who?	What kind of business?	What are the problems?
Example 1:	Rob-Fr chef	Café, brkfst + lnch	

	Who?	What kind of business?	What are the problems?
Example 2:	_____	_____	
Example 3:	_____	_____	no $, 2 yng chl, wife made him choose fam or bus

AFTER YOU LISTEN

I **THINK CRITICALLY** **Interpret an Infographic.** Work with a partner. Look at the infographic and answer the questions below.

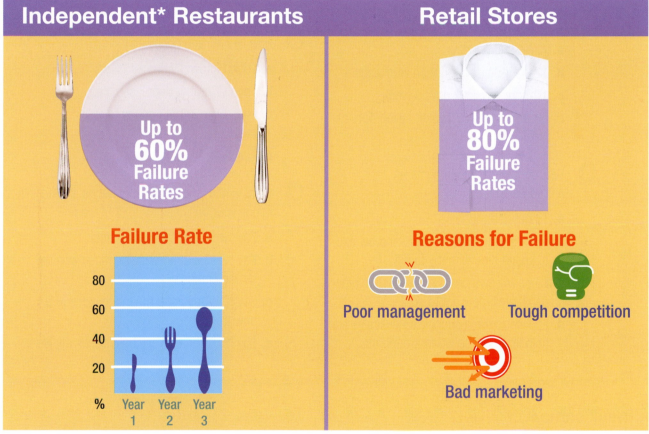

Most Likely to Fail

Independent* Restaurants

Up to **60%** Failure Rates

Failure Rate

80
60
40
20
% Year 1 Year 2 Year 3

Retail Stores

Up to **80%** Failure Rates

Reasons for Failure

Poor management   Tough competition

Bad marketing

*An independent restaurant is not part of a restaurant chain.
The owner typically works at the restaurant.

Source: thecareercafe.co.uk

1. According to the infographic, what is the failure rate for retail stores, and why do so many of them fail?

2. What percentage of independent restaurants fail within the first year? Why do you think so many restaurants fail?

3. Do you know anyone who owns or works for an independent restaurant or a retail store? If so, do they enjoy their work? Why, or why not?

J Take the quiz. Choose your answer to each question.

Would you make a good entrepreneur?

1 How much risk do you feel comfortable with?

    a. None

    b. Very little

    c. A lot, but only when necessary

    d. A lot. Taking risks is really exciting!

2 How much work would you be prepared to put into your new business?

    a. A few hours a day

    b. 12-hour days, but not on weekends

    c. 10-hour days, six days a week

    d. Every minute I'm awake, seven days a week

3 Why do you want to become an entrepreneur?

    a. To get rich

    b. To make my own schedule and be able to spend time with my family

    c. To be my own boss; I hate it when other people tell me what to do.

    d. I'd love to run a successful business and help improve the world around me.

4 How good are you with money?

    a. I have a lot of debt.

    b. I love to save money.

    c. I don't have any savings, but I don't have any debt either.

    d. I watch my money carefully; I always know how much I have and how much I owe.

5 How well do you deal with failure?

    a. I don't know; I've never failed.

    b. I don't like it. It depresses me.

    c. I don't like it, but I do my best to move on.

    d. Failure is an opportunity to learn.

6 What would you do if you someone offered to buy your business for a lot of money?

    a. Say "yes" and never work again

    b. Say "yes" and agree to continue working for the company

    c. Say "yes" and use the money to start a new business

    d. Say "no" because my business is my life

K **THINK CRITICALLY** **Analyze.** Work in a small group. Discuss these questions.

1. Based on what you heard in the podcast and your own experience, how do you think a successful entrepreneur would probably answer each quiz question?

2. Compare your answers on the quiz. Which people in your group do you think would make the best entrepreneurs? Why?

3. Discuss your answers to question number 1 with the class.

SPEAKING

SPEAKING SKILL Use a Story Example

Speakers often use stories to illustrate their main points. If you tell a story to illustrate a main point, include only information that directly supports that main point. You can follow this pattern:

- State the main point.
- Use a signal to begin your story example, such as *I have a story....., You know the story, right?* (See the Listening Skill box on page 8 for more examples.)
- Tell the story.
- Restate the main point.

L THINK CRITICALLY Support Ideas. Choose one of the main points below. Think of a story to illustrate that point. Take notes to help you remember the story. It can be a real or an imagined story. Include only information that directly supports the main point.

1. Starting your own business can be risky.

2. Owning a business can be hard on your health.

3. Working and going to school at the same time is difficult.

M COMMUNICATE Work with a partner. Follow the pattern in the Speaking Skill box and take turns telling your story examples. Don't forget to restate the main point at the end.

Intonation is the way your voice rises and falls when you speak. A pause is a short stop in the flow of speech.

In statements, speakers often use rising intonation to show that a sentence is not yet complete. Falling intonation and a brief pause are used to show that the sentence is complete. Read and listen to the example. The syllables in bold are the stressed syllables in each phrase, where the rising or falling pattern starts.

🎧 **1.8**

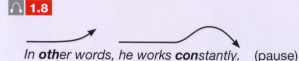

*In **oth**er words, he works **con**stantly.*   (pause)

In longer sentences, speakers often use rising intonation at the end of each phrase and falling intonation at the end of the sentence. Read and listen to the example.

*__**These** days, it seems to me that **ev**eryone is starting, or **think**ing about starting,__*

*__their own **bus**iness.__*   (pause)

These are common patterns in English, but not every speaker uses intonation in exactly the same way. However, if you use these patterns, people will understand you better.

N 🎧 **1.9** Listen to the excerpt from the podcast and read along silently. Write a slash (/) where you hear a pause. Write an upward arrow (⟋) where you hear rising intonation and a downward arrow (⟍) where you hear falling intonation. Use a straight line (——) for the parts of the sentence where the intonation is even, or flat.

Warning: This is not a reality TV show. It is just plain reality.

First, running a business is hard work. Really hard work. One hundred hours a week of hard work. — At least.

Seven days a week of hard work. No kidding. Just ask Robert.

Robert is a French chef who owns a café serving breakfast and lunch.

O 🎧 **1.9** Listen to the excerpt again and say the lines with the speaker. Then with a partner, take turns reading the sentences. Use intonation and pauses according to your markings.

P **THINK CRITICALLY** **Analyze.** Work with a partner. Discuss these questions.

1. Compare your markings from exercise N. If your answers differ, ask your teacher to play the excerpt again.

2. What effect did the intonation and the pauses have on you? Did they make it easier for you to understand the speaker?

5 ways to kill your dreams

" If you have dreams, it's your responsibility to make them happen. "

BEFORE YOU WATCH

A **COMMUNICATE** Read the title and information about the TED speaker. What is strange about the title? Discuss your ideas with your class.

BEL PESCE Entrepreneur and Author

Bel Pesce, an entrepreneur and writer, has worked at big companies including Microsoft, Google, and Deutsche Bank and has helped start several businesses. But now Pesce is looking to inspire others. She has opened a school in Brazil, FazINOVA, which is dedicated to helping students achieve their dreams. Pesce is also the author of three books and has been named one of the "100 most influential people of Brazil" by *Época* magazine.

Bel Pesce's idea worth spreading is that we are more likely to achieve our dreams if we follow five basic principles.

B **THINK CRITICALLY** **Predict.** Based on the title of Pesce's TED Talk and the information about her on page 13, what advice do you think she will give in her talk? Write three ideas in your notebook.

C **COLLABORATE** Work with a partner. Compare and discuss your answers from exercise B. Then together, make a new list of the five pieces of advice you think Pesce will give. Write your list in your notebook. Then share your list with the class.

VOCABULARY

D 🎧 **1.10** These sentences will help you learn words in the TED Talk. Read and listen to the sentences. Then choose the meaning of each bold word.

1. Some of my ideas in exercise B **overlapped** with my partner's, but some were different.
   Overlap means:
   a. be better
   b. be more difficult
   c. be similar

2. He comes from a **humble** background. Neither of his parents graduated from high school. Despite this, he became a very successful businessman.
   Humble means:
   a. inspiring
   b. modest, not rich
   c. unusual

3. When he read the university catalogue, he was excited about the large number of course offerings. He felt that he could study anything; his choices seemed **infinite**!
   Infinite means:
   a. limitless
   b. specific
   c. very interesting

4. After finally achieving her dream of opening a new bakery, she had to close it after a year because she wasn't bringing in enough **revenue** to support her family.
   Revenue means:
   a. customers
   b. money from a business
   c. savings

5. The director's first movie, *Fear*, was so successful that they made a **sequel**, *Fear II*.
   Sequel means:
   a. a book, movie, etc., that continues the story of a previous one
   b. a book, movie, etc., that is a modern version of an older one
   c. a product that is sold to promote a book, movie, etc.

6. Most professional athletes, such as tennis players, reach their **peak** when they are in their 20s or 30s. That is when they are most competitive.
   In this context, **peak** means:
   a. end of (one's) career
   b. point of greatest success
   c. top of a mountain

7. People often say that life is about the **journey**, not the final destination.
   Journey means:
   a. a long trip
   b. a visit to a special place
   c. something you write about

8. Be careful where you walk. The ground is uneven. I don't want you to **trip**.
   Trip means:
   a. to lose one's balance by stepping badly
   b. to step in water and slip
   c. to step on something sharp

9. If you go to business school, you are not **guaranteed** a good job when you graduate, but your chances are better.
   Guaranteed means:
   a. given
   b. graded
   c. promised

10. I made more money in my **prior** job, but I prefer this one.
    Prior means:
    a. earlier, previous
    b. later
    c. worse

E **COMMUNICATE** Read the statements. Check [✓] the ones you agree with. Then work with a partner and compare and explain your answers.

   A: *I disagree with number 1. In my opinion, sequels are usually not as good as the originals.*
   B: *I agree with you. Movie studios just make sequels to make more money. They don't really care about the quality of the movie.*

1. _____ Movie **sequels** are usually better than the originals.

2. _____ If you work hard, success is **guaranteed**.

3. _____ Most people reach their **peak** professionally by the age of 35.

4. _____ The **journey** is as important as the final destination.

5. _____ My **prior** teacher was excellent.

WATCH

F ▶ **1.2** **WATCH FOR MAIN IDEAS** Watch the TED Talk *5 ways to kill your dreams* by Bel Pesce. Check [✓] the statements that Pesce would agree with.

1. _____ Overnight success is the best kind of success.

2. __NO__ Let other people make decisions for you.

3. _____ When you become successful, set an even higher goal for yourself.

4. _____ Many entrepreneurs fail because they do not take responsibility for their own mistakes.

5. _____ Make sure you take time to celebrate when you are successful.

6. _____ The goal is the most important thing.

Climbers celebrating at the top of Bertha's Tower in Antarctica

G ▶ **1.3** **WATCH FOR DETAILS** Watch each segment of the TED Talk. Answer the questions.

Segment 1

1. How did Pesce get into MIT? _____

Segment 2

2. When Pesce says, "*The pipes are infinite and you're going to bump your head, and it's a part of the process,*" what do the pipes represent? _____

3. What does she mean by "*bump your head*"? _____

4. What is the process she is referring to? _____

Segment 3

5. Was Pesce's first book successful? _____

6. Why did she decide to visit every state in Brazil to promote her second book?

_____

Segment 4

7. According to Pesce, if you don't find an investor or a buyer for your product or idea, whose fault is it? _____

8. What should you do when you meet a goal? _____

H ▶ **1.4** **IDENTIFY EXAMPLES** Watch segment 1 again. Write the signals Pesce uses to introduce the two stories she tells. Then watch it one more time, and take notes on each story. The first one has been started for you. Do not write full sentences.

SIGNAL	NOTES ON STORY
	-tech guy, built mobl app

I **COMMUNICATE** Work with a partner. One student retells the first story from exercise H, and the other student retells the second story. Use the signals and your notes from the chart.

J ▶ **1.5** **EXPAND YOUR VOCABULARY** Watch the excerpts from the TED Talk. Guess the meanings of the phrases in the box.

> everything is set   the market   good talent   made it   turn into   for sure

AFTER YOU WATCH

K **COMMUNICATE** Work with a partner. Discuss your answers to these questions.

1. What is unusual about the way Pesce presents her idea worth spreading?

2. Did you find this way of presenting interesting? Why, or why not?

3. Have you personally had any experiences like those Pesce describes in her talk? Share them with your partner.

4. Do you agree with Pesce's main points? Which ones? Why, or why not?

L **THINK CRITICALLY** **Reflect.** Work in a small group. Discuss these questions.

1. Bel Pesce is a non-native speaker of English and does not pronounce every word perfectly. However, her presentation is very clear. Why? What factors contribute to the clarity of her presentation? Write a list of factors in your notebook.

2. Compare your list with those of the other groups in the class. How could you use some of the factors from question 1 to make your English clearer?

Put It Together

A THINK CRITICALLY Synthesize. Work with a partner. Complete the Venn diagram with the main points from the podcast in Part 1 and the main points from the TED Talk in Part 2. Write the main points that are shared by both in the overlapping area of the diagram.

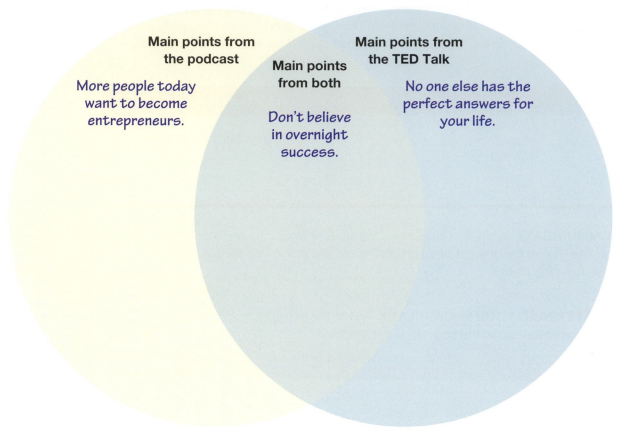

Main points from the podcast

More people today want to become entrepreneurs.

Main points from both

Don't believe in overnight success.

Main points from the TED Talk

No one else has the perfect answers for your life.

B THINK CRITICALLY Apply. Work in a small group. Discuss these questions.

1. Compare the main points you wrote in the overlapping section of your Venn diagram in exercise A. Then discuss how the podcast and TED Talk support each of these main points.

2. What dreams or goals do you have?

3. How can you apply the ideas from the podcast and/or the TED Talk to your own life?

4. How can you apply the ideas from the TED Talk to your goal of learning English?

COMMUNICATE

ASSIGNMENT: Give an Individual Presentation You will give a three-minute presentation called "How NOT to learn a foreign language." Review the ideas in Parts 1 and 2 and the listening and speaking skills as you prepare your presentation.

PREPARE

PRESENTATION SKILL Pause Effectively

Pauses can be very effective when you give an oral presentation. They give the audience time to adjust to your voice and to process information.

Watch the excerpts from the TED Talk and notice the three ways that the speaker uses pauses effectively. Please note that these are not rules, but rather guidelines for pausing.

▶ 1.6

Pause after introducing a main point.

Believe the fault is someone else's. (pause) *I constantly see people saying . . .*
(main point)

Pause before moving from an example to a restatement of the main idea.

I constantly see people saying, "Yes, I had this great idea . . ."
(long example)

(pause) *If you have dreams, it's your responsibility to make them happen.* (pause)
(restatement of main point)

Pause before moving on to your next main point.

Be responsible for your dreams. (pause) *And one last tip, and this one is really*
(main point)   *important as well . . .*
(next main point)

When preparing for a presentation, it helps to think about when you are going to pause. You might even write *PAUSE* in your notes.

Employees at a small business take a moment to celebrate a success.

C ▶ **1.7** Review the Pronunciation Skill box on page 12 and the Presentation Skill box on page 19. Watch the excerpt from the TED Talk and read along. Pay attention to how and where Bel Pesce uses pauses. Write a slash (/) to indicate a pause. Then work with a partner and compare your markings.

And one last tip,/and this one is really important as well:/Believe that the only things that matter are the dreams themselves./Once I saw an ad,/and it was a lot of friends, they were going up a mountain, it was a very high mountain, and it was a lot of work,/You could see that they were sweating and this was tough. And they were going up, and they finally made it to the peak./Of course, they decided to celebrate, right? I'm going to celebrate, so, "Yes! We made it, we're at the top!" Two seconds later,/one looks at the other and says, "Okay, let's go down." Life is never about the goals themselves. Life is about the journey.

D COLLABORATE Work in a small group. Discuss things that you did that did NOT work well when you were trying to learn a foreign language (English or another language). Take notes on your classmates' ideas.

E **THINK CRITICALLY** **Support Ideas.** Follow these steps:

- Review your notes from exercise D and think about your own experience learning a foreign language.

- Identify three main points to include in your presentation.

- Think of a story example to support each main point.

- Prepare notes for your presentation. Do *not* write full sentences. Include reminders to pause at certain points in your presentation.

F Read the rubric on page 179. Notice how your presentation will be evaluated. Keep these categories in mind as you present and watch your classmates' presentations.

PRESENT

G Give your presentation to the class. Watch your classmates' presentations. After you watch each one, provide feedback using the rubric as a guide. Add notes or any other feedback you want to share.

H **THINK CRITICALLY** **Evaluate.** In your group, discuss the feedback you received. Discuss what you did well and what might make your presentation even stronger.

REFLECT

Reflect on what you have learned. Check [✓] your progress.

I can
- [ ] listen for main points and examples.
- [ ] take notes using abbreviations.
- [ ] tell a story that directly supports a main point.
- [ ] use rising and falling intonation correctly.
- [ ] use pauses effectively.

I understand the meanings of these words and phrases and can use them.
Circle those you know. Underline those you need to work on.

bankruptcy	humble	overnight success	sequel
catch up on	infinite AWL	peak	settle down
constantly AWL	investor AWL	prior AWL	striking
estimate AWL	journey	revenue AWL	trip
guarantee AWL	overlap AWL	run a business	wealth

UNIT **2**
Say It Your Way

Tunisian artist eL Seed's mural at Djerbahood, an open air public museum on the streets of Erriadh, Djerba, Tunisia

THINK AND DISCUSS

1 Do you find it easy to express yourself orally? How about in writing? Explain your answers.

2 Read the unit title. What do you think "Say It Your Way" means? How do you think the photo relates to the unit title?

23

PART 1 Emoji and Emoticons:  or 👎?

BEFORE YOU LISTEN

A COMMUNICATE Work in a small group. Discuss these questions.

1. Look at the photo. Are you familiar with emoji and emoticons? Why do people use them?

2. In which of the following ways do you communicate with your friends? Estimate the average number of times a day that you use each method and write it on the line. Then compare your answers with your classmates'.

> _____ text messages   _____ email   _____ telephone calls
>
> _____ Snapchat   _____ Instagram   _____ Other _____
>
> _____ Tweets   _____ messages on Facebook

3. Do you often use emoticons or emoji when you communicate with your friends? Why, or why not?

B THINK CRITICALLY Predict. The title of the podcast you are going to listen to is _Emoji and Emoticons: 👍 or 👎?_ In a group, discuss the meaning of the title. What do you think the podcast will be about? Write your ideas in your notebook.

VOCABULARY

C 🎧 **1.11** Read and listen to the sentences with words and phrases from the podcast. Guess the meaning of each bold word or phrase. Then match each word or phrase to its definition.

a. Thousands of years ago, before there were any written languages, our human **ancestors** used pictures and **symbols** to communicate. Even with just simple symbols and pictures, they managed to communicate **complex** messages.

b. In addition to spoken language, all human beings also use body language to help them **get across** their ideas. The use of body language, which includes both **gestures** with your hands and **facial expressions**, such as a smile, is **universal**.

c. English has a lot of **compound** words for weather. Two examples include *sunlight* (*sun + light*) and *snowstorm* (*snow + storm*).

d. In informal conversation in English, **reductions** are quite common. For example, *going to* sounds like *gonna*, and *have to* sounds like *hafta*.

e. With the Internet, it is easy to **spread** information from one side of the world to the other in just minutes.

1. _reductions_ — (n) shortened forms of a phrase

2. _get across_ — (phrasal v) communicate

3. _ancestors_ — (n) family members who lived a very long time ago, for example our great-great-great grandparents

4. _gestures_ — (n) body movements to show something, such as a feeling

5. _compound_ — (adj) made by combining two or more things

6. _complex_ — (adj) not simple; complicated

7. _universal_ — (adj) found or practiced everywhere

8. _facial expressions_ — (n) the looks on people's faces

9. _symbols_ — (n) signs, marks, pictures, or objects understood to represent something else

10. _spread_ — (v) to go or travel a distance and reach many people

Two men play checkers in the High Atlas Mountains, Morocco.

D COMMUNICATE Work with a partner. Read and answer the questions. Use the bold words and phrases in your answers.

> A: *Is it easier for you to **get** your feelings **across** when you are talking to someone face-to-face or when you are texting?*
>
> B: *Hmmm. Interesting question. I guess it depends on who I'm talking to. With someone I know very well, it's easier **to get** my feelings **across** face-to-face. But when I don't know someone very well, I prefer to text.*

1. Is it easier for you to **get** your feelings **across** when you are talking to someone face-to-face, or when you can't see the person; for example, when you are texting? Explain why.

2. What are some **compound** words in English? List at least five.

3. In your culture, do most parents teach their children about their **ancestors**? What do you know about your **ancestors**?

4. How important are **facial expressions** to human communication? Do you think **facial expressions** are becoming less important these days than in the past? Why, or why not?

5. Do you think most **gestures** are **universal**, or do they vary from culture to culture? Show your partner some common **gestures** from your culture (e.g., gestures used to communicate ideas, such as "good," "OK," "I don't know," or "wait"). Are the **gestures** from your two cultures similar or different?

6. If you needed to **spread** information quickly to a large group of people, how would you do it? Why would you use this method?

LISTEN

E 🎧 **1.12** ▶ **1.8** **LISTEN FOR MAIN IDEAS** Read the statements. Then listen to the podcast. Check [✓] the two sentences that express the contrasting points of view that the podcast host wants her listeners to consider.

1. _____ Emoji and emoticons are less direct than written words.

2. _____ Emoji and emoticons help people to communicate better.

3. _____ Emoji and emoticons express universal human feelings.

4. _____ Emoji and emoticons are harming written language.

F Go back and check your predictions from exercise B on page 24. Were any of them correct?

G 🎧 **1.12** **LISTEN FOR DETAILS** Read the questions below. Then listen to the podcast again and put the questions in the order the podcast host answers them. Write *1* next to the first question she answers, *2* next to the second, and so on. The first one has been done for you.

a. _____ Why do some people criticize the use of emoticons and emoji?

b. ___1___ What are emoticons?

c. _____ Why have emoji and emoticons spread all over the world?

d. _____ How do emoji and emoticons make written communication more like speaking?

e. _____ Why do some people support the use of emoticons and emoji?

f. _____ What are emoji and how were they invented?

WORDS IN THE PODCAST
a locust (n): an insect of the grasshopper family noted for flying in large groups and destroying crops
pollinate (v): to transfer pollen from one plant to another so that it can reproduce

A Filipino farmer uses a fishnet tied to a stick to catch a swarm of locusts devastating rice fields.

LISTENING SKILL Listen for Explanations of Words and Terms

When you listen to learn about a specific topic, you will often hear some unfamiliar words and terms. Listening for explanations of content-specific words and terms will help you better understand both the new vocabulary and the speaker's ideas. Here are some common types of explanations to listen for:

A definition of the word or term

Emoji are small, cartoon-like pictures of just about anything—from a doghouse to a watermelon.

An analogy: an explanation of how a word or term is similar to something else

Emoji and emoticons are like pictures scratched on rocks.

A description of the word's or term's function or purpose

Emoticons express both feelings and ideas in online communication.

An explanation of how the word or term is formed

The word emoticon *is a combination of two words:* emotion *and* icon.

An example of the word or term

An icon *is a type of symbol, such as a drawing of a heart broken into two pieces to mean* heartbroken.

H 🎧 **1.13** Listen to the segments of the podcast. Pay close attention to the explanations of the words and terms. Then answer the questions.

Segment 1

1. What are emoticons? _emotion + icon - express feelings_

2. What are emoticons made from? _Japan / Scott Thornton_

3. What is a compound word? _combination between 2 words_

4. What is one example of a compound word? _blending gonna_

5. What does the *e-* in *emoji* mean? _picture_

6. What does *moji* mean? _small pictures use to create sentences_

Segment 2

7. The podcast host compares emoji and emoticons to "pictures scratched on rocks." What else does she compare them to? _____

Segment 3

8. What does the podcast host say that a reduction in formal speech is similar to?

   _____

9. What is one example? _____

Speakers often give a lot of explanations, but when you take notes, you will not have time to write everything down. Focus on writing down the main points. Write an explanation only if it helps you to understand the main point.

Here are some notes that answer the first question in exercise H. Notice how only some of the explanations are recorded.

> What are emoticons?
>
> *simple pics made fr punct & othr symb : -)*

(See page 168 of the *Independent Student Handbook* for more information on condensing information in your notes.)

I 🎧 **1.14** Listen to the segment from the podcast and take notes under the questions. Write only enough information to answer the questions.

1. Why do some people criticize the use of emoticons and emoji?

   losing the abetily and comunicatson

2. Why do some people support the use of emoticons and emoji?

   improve facial expresiont add mirrors -

McKee Springs petroglyphs (pictures scratched on rocks), Dinosaur National Monument, Utah, USA

AFTER YOU LISTEN

J **THINK CRITICALLY** **Compare.** Work with a partner. Use your notes to take turns answering the questions from exercise I on page 29. As you listen to your partner's answers, ask yourself the questions below. Then compare your notes and discuss why you recorded what you did.

1. Did my partner write down the same kind and amount of information that I did?

2. If not, how are our notes different?

K **COLLABORATE** Work with a partner. Read the emoji messages and try to figure out what they mean. Write a "translation" for each message. Then share your ideas with the class.

1.

2.

3.

4.

5.

6.

L Check your answers from exercise K on page 178. How many messages did you translate correctly?

SPEAKING

M Work with a partner. Take turns pronouncing the compound words in the Pronunciation Skill box. If your partner makes a mistake, correct him or her.

N **COMMUNICATE** Work with a partner. Take turns explaining the bold words and terms below, using the techniques in parentheses. Make sure you pronounce the compound words correctly.

1. **compound word:** (Give a definition. Then give a few examples.)

2. **watermelon:** (Explain how this word is formed. Then give its definition.)

3. **doghouse:** (Describe its purpose.)

4. **honeybee:** (Explain how this word is formed. Then give its definition.)

A honeybee pollinating a flower

Go ahead, make up new words

“ My job is not to decide what a word is; that's your job. ”

BEFORE YOU WATCH

A   COMMUNICATE Read the title and information about the TED speaker. Then with a partner, answer the questions below.

> ### ERIN MCKEAN   Lexicographer
>
> Erin McKean is a lexicographer; she writes dictionaries. She searches for words everywhere—from books and blogs, to parties and Twitter feeds. She recently started *Wordnik*, an online dictionary that contains all the traditionally accepted words and definitions, but also asks users to contribute new words and new uses for old words. McKean is also an active blogger and the author of many books, including the *Weird and Wonderful Words* series.
>
> Erin McKean's idea worth spreading is that making up new words will help us use language to express what we mean and will create new ways for us to understand one another.

1. What does it mean to *make up* a new word? Have you ever made up any new words, either in English or in your native language?

2. What is a lexicographer?

3. Do new words appear in your language every year? If so, where do you think they come from? Who do you think creates them?

4. Give an example of a new word in your native language. Translate it for your partner. Why do you think this new word appeared in your language?

B **THINK CRITICALLY Predict.** Read the list of topics below. Check [✓] the topics you think the talk will include. Then with a partner, compare and discuss your answers.

1. _____   how dictionary writers decide which words to put in the dictionary

2. _____   how new words are created in English

3. _____   who creates new words in a language

4. _____   why McKean decided to become a lexicographer

VOCABULARY

C 🎧 **1.16** The sentences below will help you learn words and phrases in the edited TED Talk. Read and listen to the sentences. Guess the meaning of each bold word or phrase. Then choose the best meaning.

1. Our use of our native language is **unconscious**. We are not aware of the grammar rules, but we can still speak correctly.
   a. incorrect   **b.** understandable   **c.** without thinking

2. People with good **manners** use polite language. They do not use rude or abusive terms.
   a. background   **b.** social behavior   **c.** vocabulary

3. People who write dictionaries are usually **linguists**. When they are at university, they study how languages work.
   a. hard workers   **b.** language experts   **c.** teachers

4. Word **usage** changes over time. For example, before Facebook existed, *friend* was only used as a noun. However, it is now used as a verb.
   a. definitions   **b.** pronunciation   **c.** how something is used

5. We should not **discourage** children from using language in creative ways. We should support their creativity.

    a. help

    b. make a mistake

    c. take away (someone's) confidence

6. Don't **squish** all of your words on the same line! It makes your writing very difficult to read.

    a. copy neatly

    b. put closely together

    c. spell incorrectly

7. Unusual words **grab** people's **attention**. When you use them, people become interested and listen carefully to you.

    a. get (someone) interested

    b. interfere with (someone's) understanding

    c. make (someone) understand better

8. The meanings of words can change over time. For example, in the 14th century, *girl* meant a female or male child. Later, there was a **shift** in meaning, and *girl* now only refers to females.

    a. change

    b. difference

    c. problem

9. Television **commercials** help companies sell products. The best ones use words and pictures in unusual ways. This helps people remember the product.

    a. advertisements

    b. pictures

    c. programs

10. The word *camcorder* is a **blend** word. It combines parts of two words—*camera* and *recorder*—to form a new word, with its own definition: a camera that can record videos.

    a. combination of two or more parts

    b. brand name

    c. compound

A man using a *camcorder* to film a volcano eruption, Holuhraun Fissure, Iceland.

D COMMUNICATE Read the statements and write a number for each according to how strongly you agree or disagree with it. Then explain your answers to a partner. Use the bold words and phrases in your explanations.

> 1 = I strongly agree.   2 = I agree.   3 = I disagree.

> A: *I "disagree" with statement number 1. I don't like watching commercials at all!*
> B: *Really? I think some commercials are funny.*

1. _____ **Commercials** that use words in clever ways are fun to watch.

2. _____ Unusual words **grab** my **attention.**

3. _____ Teachers should **discourage** their students from using slang.

4. _____ It is bad **manners** to interrupt people when they are speaking.

5. _____ **Linguists** can probably find jobs easily.

6. _____ When I speak English, I am **unconscious** of the grammar rules. I just talk.

WATCH

acuplacer

E ▶ 1.9 WATCH FOR MAIN IDEAS Watch the edited TED Talk. Check [✓] the one statement that best expresses the speaker's main purpose.

1. _____ She wants people to buy her dictionary.

2 _____ She wants people to understand how English works.

3. _____ She wants people to understand the job of a lexicographer.

4. __✗__ She wants to encourage people to be creative with language.

F ▶ 1.10 WATCH FOR DETAILS Watch the first segment of the edited TED Talk. Listen for the words and phrases in Column A of the chart. Then match each word or phrase from Column A with the correct type of example or explanation in Column B.

Segment 1

COLUMN A	COLUMN B
1. a group of people who agree to understand each other	a. Explanation(s) of what language is _a_
2. knowing how to make the plural of the invented word *wug*	b. Examples used to explain what natural grammar rules are _2, 3, 5_
3. not like traffic rules	
4. manners	c. Examples used to explain what usage rules are _4, 6_
5. the law of gravity	
6. knowing that you wear a hat on your head and not on your feet	

G ▶ **1.11** **WATCH FOR DETAILS** Watch the remaining segments of the edited TED Talk. Are the sentences true or false, according to the talk? Write T for *true* or F for *false*.

Segment 2

1. _____T_____ It is fun to make up new words in English.

2. _____F_____ The speaker thinks that English has too many words.

Segment 3

3. _____T_____ A lot of words in English come from other languages.

4. _____F_____ *Heartbroken* is an example of a blend word.

5. _____T_____ Nouns in English often become verbs.

6. _____F_____ The word *edit* existed before the word *editor*.

H ▶ **1.12** **LISTEN FOR EXPLANATIONS OF WORDS AND TERMS** Read the words and terms and their explanations below. Then watch the segments of the TED Talk. What kind of explanation(s) does the speaker use? Write the letter of the type of explanation. You will need to use some explanations more than once.

Segment 1: lexicographer _____

Segment 2: the grammar that lives inside your brain _____

Segment 3: compounding _____ , _____ , _____

Segment 4: blending _____ , _____

Explanations

a. Define what the word or term means or what it is.

b. Say what the word or term is similar to. This is called an analogy.

c. Describe what it does or what its purpose is.

d. Explain how this type of word or term is formed or was created.

e. Give an example of the word or term.

I **EXPLAIN WORDS AND TERMS** Work with a partner. Take turns explaining the meanings of the words and terms in the box. How was each word or term made? Match each word or term with the correct linguistic term from the talk.

> boutique (n)   email (n)   to flame (v)
> LOL   thunderstorm (n)

SXMB

create a new word

1. borrowing _boutic_
2. compounding _thunderstorm,_
3. blending _email (electr. mail_
4. functional shift _to flame_
5. put first letters of several words together to form a new word _LOL._

J ▶ **1.13** **EXPAND YOUR VOCABULARY** Watch the excerpts from the TED Talk. Guess the meanings of the phrases in the box.

> laws of nature   give it a rest   go ahead
> as opposed to   makes no sense

K **WATCH MORE** Go to TED.com to watch the full TED Talk by Erin McKean.

A *boutique* in Vancouver, Canada

AFTER YOU WATCH

L THINK CRITICALLY **Interpret an Infographic.** Work in a small group. Look at the infographic and discuss the answers to the questions on page 39.

How a New Word Gets into a Traditional Dictionary

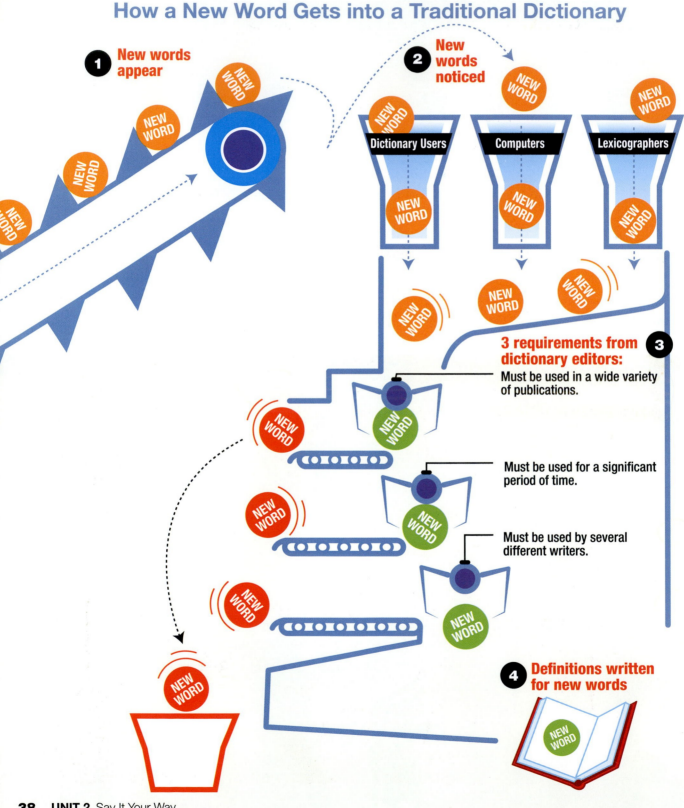

1 New words appear

2 New words noticed

Dictionary Users

Computers

Lexicographers

3 requirements from dictionary editors:

Must be used in a wide variety of publications.

Must be used for a significant period of time.

Must be used by several different writers.

4 Definitions written for new words

1. Who or what is involved in finding new words to add to a dictionary?

2. What requirements must a word meet to be included in a dictionary? Why do you think all three of these requirements are important?

3. Who is in charge of making sure new words meet all three of the requirements?

4. What happens after a new word meets all three requirements?

M THINK CRITICALLY Infer. Work in a small group. Discuss the answers to these questions.

1. Who do you think notices more new words: dictionary users or lexicographers? Why?

2. How long do you estimate the process of adding a word to a dictionary took in the past? Days? Months? Years? How long does it take today? Explain your answers.

3. How do you think the process Erin McKean uses for her own online dictionary, *Wordnik*, is different from the process shown in the infographic in exercise L?

4. Based on the process shown in the infographic for adding new words to traditional dictionaries and what you have learned about Erin McKean, why do you think she decided to start her own online dictionary?

Kumquat trees being delivered for Tet Nguyen Dan or Vietnamese Lunar New Year festival, Hanoi, Vietnam. *Kumquat* **is an example of a borrowed word that is now part of the English language.**

A THINK CRITICALLY Synthesize. Work in a small group. Discuss these questions.

1. Would Erin McKean be in favor of using emoji and emoticons in texting and email?

2. Would she agree that they are more like "*word-eating locusts that will end up killing the written word*" or more like "*honeybees that pollinate our writing and allow us to grow our ideas and spread them over large distances*"? Explain your opinion by referring to comments McKean makes during her edited TED Talk, as well as her biography.

COMMUNICATE

ASSIGNMENT: Give a Pair Presentation You and a partner are going to present and teach new words to your classmates. Review the ideas in Parts 1 and 2 and the listening and speaking skills as you prepare your presentation.

PREPARE

PRESENTATION SKILL **Encourage Audience Participation**

In an interactive presentation, the speaker encourages the audience to participate. This can help make the presentation more fun and more memorable. Here are some ways to help the audience feel comfortable enough to participate.

- Be relaxed and friendly—smile! It will make the audience feel more comfortable and make them more likely to participate.

- Ask questions.

- Prepare follow-up questions in case no one answers.

- Engage in a positive, encouraging way with audience members who do answer—even when their answers are not correct.

- At the end of the presentation, thank your audience for listening and participating.

Language to Encourage Participation

Maria, how about you? Do you want to give it a try?

Let me give you a hint. (Hint = Give them part of the answer, for example, *The first part means X. Now can you guess?*)

Does anybody else have a different idea?

Great, thank you. Any other guesses?

B COLLABORATE Work with a partner. Make up two to four new words for Erin McKean's online dictionary, *Wordnik*. Use at least two of the techniques for making up new words that McKean teaches—borrowing, compounding, blending, functional shift, back formation—or make a new word with the first letters of several words. Make up a clear explanation for each new word.

C Prepare for your presentation. Follow these steps:

1. Write your words and the name of the technique you used to make each word up.

2. Decide on the order of your words and who will present each word.

3. Decide on the best type(s) of explanations to use when explaining the words. Use more than one technique for each word, e.g., an analogy and a definition.

4. Practice your presentation with your partner. Follow these steps:
   - Present each word. Ask your classmates to guess the meaning. Use the information in the Presentation Skill box to encourage participation.
   - If your classmates guess the meaning, praise them and give your explanation.
   - If your classmates can't guess the meaning, give them a hint. If they still can't guess it, give your explanation and move on to the next word.

D Read the rubric on page 179. Notice how your pair presentation will be evaluated. Keep these categories in mind as you present and watch your classmates' presentations.

PRESENT

E Give your pair presentation to the class. Watch other pairs' presentations. After you watch each one, provide feedback using the rubric as a guide. Add notes or any other feedback you want to share.

F **THINK CRITICALLY** **Evaluate.** With your partner, discuss the feedback you received. Discuss what you did well and what might make your presentation even stronger.

REFLECT

Reflect on what you have learned. Check [✓] your progress.

I can
- [ ] listen for explanations of words and terms.
- [ ] focus on and write down only main points.
- [ ] explain words and terms.
- [ ] pronounce compound words correctly.
- [ ] encourage audience participation.

I understand the meanings of these words and phrases and can use them.
Circle those you know. Underline those you need to work on.

ancestor	discourage	linguist	squish
blend	facial expression	manners	symbol AWL
commercial	gesture	reduction	unconscious
complex AWL	get across	shift	universal
compound AWL	grab attention	spread	usage

To the Rescue!

New York City firefighters use an emergency staircase to evacuate passengers from a derailed train in Queens, New York, USA.

THINK AND DISCUSS

1 Look at the photo. What do you think happened before it was taken? What is happening in the photo?

2 Read the unit title. What do you think the unit is going to be about?

PART 1 Animal Heroes

BEFORE YOU LISTEN

A COMMUNICATE Work in a small group. Discuss these questions.

1. Look at the photo. What is happening? How does the photo relate to the unit title?

2. Read the title of Part 1. Why would someone call an animal a *hero*? Have you ever heard of an animal doing something heroic? Tell your group about it.

B THINK CRITICALLY Predict. Work in a small group. Discuss these questions and predict the answers that you will hear in the lecture.

1. What does *search and rescue* mean? In what situations are search and rescue missions necessary?

2. In what ways do animals help humans? Be specific.

3. What kinds of animals will the lecturer probably mention?

A dog trained in avalanche rescue, Fernie, British Columbia

VOCABULARY

C 🎧 **1.17** Read and listen to the sentences with words from the lecture. Guess the meaning of each bold word. Then write each word next to its definition.

a. Police and firemen are usually the first **responders** to a disaster.

b. There were only five **survivors** of the plane crash. Everyone else died.

c. Experts are always looking for better ways to respond to a disaster. They are open to **innovative** ideas that no one has ever thought of before.

d. The **sensors** in the latest fire alarms work very well. They can detect the presence of smoke immediately.

e. When you **activate** the fire alarm, the elevators stop working immediately.

f. To remember and respect those who died in the fire, the town placed a statue on the **site** where the building burned down.

g. In a fire, elevators are automatically locked and people are unable to **access** them. That is because it is very dangerous to use an elevator during a fire.

h. The whole town was **devastated** by the fire. Almost everyone knew someone who was injured or died.

i. It is dangerous to go into the **wilderness** alone. You could be attacked by a wild animal or fall down and injure yourself, and no one would be able to find you.

j. You should never **underestimate** the power of the ocean. It might look very beautiful, but it can suddenly become extremely dangerous.

1. _____ (v) completely destroyed

2. _____ (v) guess that someone or something's capability is less than it actually is

3. _____ (adj) newly made or improved with creativity

4. _____ (n) people who survive a life-threatening event

5. _____ (n) machines for sensing (heat, movement, light, etc.)

6. _____ (v) enter; go into

7. _____ (v) put in motion; start

8. _____ (n) people who come to help when there is a serious accident or disaster

9. _____ (n) an area or place

10. _____ (n) land in its natural state, especially a large area where humans rarely or never go

D **COMMUNICATE** Work in pairs. Answer the questions. Use the words in **bold** in your answers.

> A: *I love spending time in the **wilderness** because I like to escape from city life.*
>
> B: *I am more of a city person. I like to look at pictures of the **wilderness**, but I don't feel comfortable going there. I guess I'm a little scared of being that far away from everything.*

1. Do you like to spend time in the **wilderness?** Why, or why not?

2. Have people ever **underestimated** you, or have you ever **underestimated** someone else? Explain what they (or you) underestimated.

3. What is an interesting story you have heard about a **survivor** of a disaster? Tell the story to your partner.

4. What kinds of everyday objects have **sensors** in them? Think of as many as you can.

5. What personality traits do you think first **responders** to disasters need to have? Would you like to be a first responder? Why, or why not?

6. When people's houses, towns, and communities have been **devastated** in a disaster, do the people ever fully recover? Why, or why not?

7. What historical **sites** have you visited? What historical event took place there?

LISTEN

E 🎧 **1.18** ▶ **1.14** **LISTEN FOR MAIN IDEAS** Listen to the lecture. Check [✓] the four topics that the lecturer discusses.

1. _____ the history of search and rescue dogs

2. _____ how search and rescue dogs are trained

3. _____ how technology could make search and rescue dogs more effective

4. _____ how rats are used to find people after a natural disaster

5. _____ why rats are good at finding landmines

6. _____ how rats are trained to help people

7. _____ how ravens can help rescue people who are buried

8. _____ why ravens might make very good rescue animals

WORDS IN THE LECTURE

geospatial (adj): describing data that is associated with a particular location
hospice (n): a place where people go to rest and recover, often after an illness
monastery (n): a place where monks live, work, and pray
monks (n): members of an all male religious order who all live together

F 🎧 **1.18** **LISTEN FOR DETAILS** Listen to the lecture again. Check [✓] the information in the chart that is true for each animal *based on the information in the lecture*. Do *not* check the information if it is not mentioned in the lecture.

	DOGS	RATS	RAVENS
1. used for hundreds of years	✓		
2. rescue people who are buried	✓		
3. find people	✓		✓
4. find landmines		✓	
5. are trainable	✓	✓	✓
6. have an excellent sense of smell	✓	✓	
7. have excellent eyesight			✓
8. form relationships with people	✓		✓
9. are faster than people		✓	✓
10. use technology		✓	✓

A Gambian giant pouch rat in a suspected minefield near the town of Vilanculos in southern Mozambique

Monks and a team of Saint Bernard dogs rescue a lost traveler in the Swiss Alps circa 1955.

LISTENING SKILL Ask Questions While Listening

Fluent listeners listen to and understand what the speaker is saying at the moment, but they also *listen ahead*. Based on the information they hear, they anticipate what kind of information is probably going to come next. One way to listen ahead is by asking simple *Wh-* questions (questions that begin with *Who, What, When, Where, How* (*much/many*), and *Why*). Read and listen to the example.

🎧 **1.19**

You hear:　　　　*Today we're going to talk about animal heroes—that is, animals that help save human lives.*

You ask yourself:　*What kinds of animals?*

The speaker's next sentence gives one answer: *Let's start with man's best friend, the dog.*

G 🎧 **1.20** Listen to the segments from the lecture. There will be a pause after each segment to give you time to write a question that you think the lecturer will answer in the next segment.

Segment 1

Your question: ___How they do it?___ ?

Segment 2

Your question: ___What is the skill?___ ?

Segment 3

Your question: _____ ?

H 🎧 **1.21** Listen to the segments from the lecture again, this time without pauses. If the lecturer answers a question you wrote in exercise G, put a check [✓] next to it.

I **COMMUNICATE** Work with a partner. Take turns asking and answering the questions you checked in exercise G.

AFTER YOU LISTEN

J **COLLABORATE** Work with a partner. Look at the chart. Discuss how dogs help people in each of the contexts. Write notes in the chart. Then talk to other pairs of students until you find some new information to add to your chart.

CONTEXT	HOW DO DOGS HELP PEOPLE?
on farms	
with the police	
with people who are disabled	
in hospitals	
in the military	
other	

SPEAKING

SPEAKING SKILL **Give Reasons**

When explaining ideas, it is important to tell not only *what* happens or happened, but also *why*. There are many words and phrases that you can use to give reasons. Here are some common ones:

because + clause (reason)

*Ravens would make good rescue animals **because** <u>they are intelligent and trainable</u>.*

due to + noun (reason)

***Due to** <u>their sense of smell,</u> dogs are able to find people buried under snow.*

in order to (often shortened to just **to**) + reason

*Technology is being used **in order to** <u>make rescue dogs even more effective.</u>*

🎧 **1.22** Read and listen to the example from the lecture.

*Monks from the St. Bernard Hospice and Monastery, located in the 49-mile St. Bernard Pass between Switzerland and Italy, kept a breed of dog with an excellent sense of direction. These dogs were very helpful **due to** the heavy snowstorms that were common in the area.*

K 🎧 **1.23** **COMMUNICATE** Work with a partner. Listen to the segments of the lecture and take turns answering the questions.

Segment 1

1. Why are people still dying years after a war is over?

Segment 2

2. Why is it safer to send in rats to find landmines than humans?

Segment 3

3. Why do people use the expression "bird brain" to refer to someone who's done something stupid?

L **THINK CRITICALLY** **Support Ideas.** Work in pairs. Look at the information in the chart in exercise J on page 49. Practice asking and answering *why* questions about the information. If you are not sure of an answer, make your best guess.

   A: *Why do farmers use dogs?*
   B: *Because they are fast and can help the farmer control other animals like sheep.*

PRONUNCIATION SKILL **Syllable Stress**

In words with two or more syllables, one syllable is stressed more than the others. If you put the stress on the wrong syllable, people may not understand the word.

To stress a syllable, make the vowel in that syllable longer and raise the pitch.

🎧 **1.24** Listen to the examples.

un-der-**es**-ti-mate   re-s**pon**-der   **in**-no-va-tive

M 🎧 **1.25** Listen and underline the stressed syllable in each word. Then with a partner, take turns pronouncing each word.

   1. ac-cess   **5.** dis-pro-ven

   2. ac-ti-vate   **6.** sen-sor

   3. av-a-lanche   **7.** sur-vi-vor

   4. dev-as-tat-ed   **8.** wild-er-ness

N **COLLABORATE** With a partner, write five sentences. In each sentence, use one of the words from exercise M. Then take turns reading the sentences. Make sure your partner stresses the correct syllable of the words from exercise M.

_____

_____

_____

_____

_____

O THINK CRITICALLY Infer. Work in pairs. Answer the questions.

1. What is an assistance dog? Give a definition based on what you see in the illustration.

2. What do you think each type of assistance dog does? Explain your answers by referring to the illustration, as well as your prior knowledge and experience.

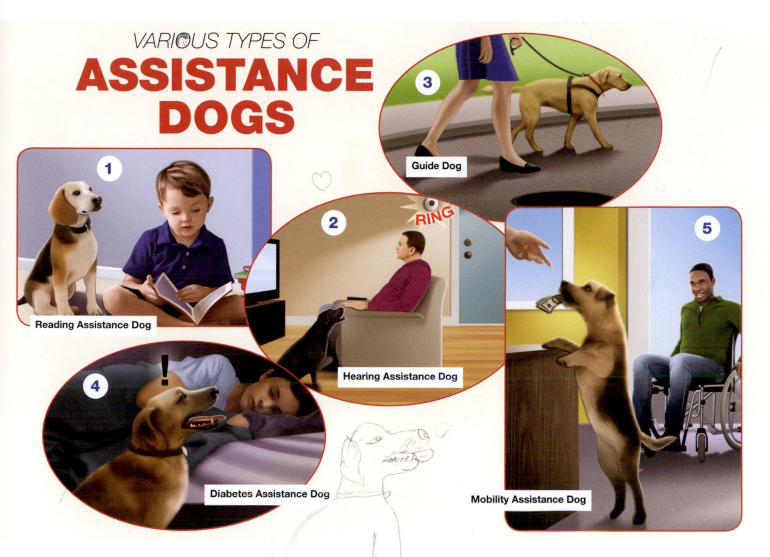

VARIOUS TYPES OF
ASSISTANCE DOGS

3 Guide Dog

1 Reading Assistance Dog

2 RING Hearing Assistance Dog

4 Diabetes Assistance Dog

5 Mobility Assistance Dog

P THINK CRITICALLY Personalize. Work in a small group. Discuss these questions.

1. Are assistance dogs common in your country? If so, what kinds are most common? Were any of the kinds of assistance dogs from the illustration new to you? If so, which ones?

2. Have you seen or had personal experience with any of the types of assistance dogs in the illustration? If so, which ones? What was your experience?

3. Would you like to help with the training of an assistance dog? Why, or why not?

PART 2 TEDTALKS

These robots come to the rescue after a disaster

> " Look for the robots, because robots are coming to the rescue. "

BEFORE YOU WATCH

A THINK CRITICALLY Predict. Read the title and the information about the TED speaker. How do you think the information in the edited TED Talk will be similar to the information in the lecture in Part 1, *Animal Heroes*? How do you think it will it be different? Discuss your ideas with a partner.

ROBIN MURPHY Disaster Roboticist

Robin Murphy is the director of the Center for Robot-Assisted Search and Rescue and the Center for Emergency Informatics at Texas A&M University. In 2014, she was awarded the ACM Eugene L. Lawler Award for Humanitarian Contributions within Computer Science and Informatics.

Robin Murphy imagines how robots can do things no human could on the scenes of disasters from hurricanes to terrorist attacks. In her recent book, *Disaster Robotics*, she explains her research, which brings together artificial intelligence, robotics, and human–robot interaction.

B COMMUNICATE Work with a partner. Look at the list of disasters. Check [✓] the ones that are common in your country. Look up any words you don't know in a dictionary.

_____ avalanche	_____ hurricane	_____ train derailment
_____ earthquake	_____ mudslide	_____ tsunami
_____ flood	_____ nuclear disaster	_____ typhoon

C THINK CRITICALLY **Predict.** Work in a small group. Answer these questions.

1. Which of the disasters from exercise B have gotten the most international media attention over the past several years? Where did they happen? Which of these disasters do you think the TED speaker will mention in her talk?

2. Read the definitions for three different categories of robots below.* How could robots be useful in the disasters in exercise B? Be specific about what the robots might be able to do in each type of disaster.

*UAV (Unmanned Aerial Vehicle), UMV (Unmanned Marine Vehicle), and UGV (Unmanned Ground Vehicle)

VOCABULARY

D 🎧 **1.26** The sentences below will help you learn words in the edited TED Talk. Read and listen to the sentences. Then choose the meanings of the words in bold.

1. When I asked him to travel with me to the site of the disaster, his **initial** response was "no." However, after a few more conversations, he finally agreed to go.
   a. best
   b. first
   c. latest

2. After a snowstorm, we sometimes lose power in my town. It can take days for the power company to **restore** it.
   a. make (something) work again
   b. replace
   c. turn off

3. Animals are often more **resilient** than humans. That is why they can recover faster from disasters and injuries.
   a. able to concentrate
   b. able to handle difficulties
   c. able to understand

4. After a disaster, insurance companies usually have to **process** claims from thousands of people who have lost property in the disaster.

   a. apply a procedure to

   b. make many copies of

   c. locate and rescue

5. If a building has **structural** problems, it could easily fall down during an earthquake.

   a. relating to air quality

   b. relating to construction

   c. relating to electricity

6. The **imagery** in the movie about the hurricane was incredible. The photos of the damaged trees and houses showed just how powerful it was.

   a. buildings

   b. sounds and feeling

   c. use of visual information

7. After a disaster, it sometimes takes a long time for a city to repair the damage to its **infrastructure** and get everything working properly again.

   a. important systems, such as highways and electricity

   b. government buildings, such as courthouses and city halls

   c. the local population; the people who live in a specific area

8. Many different types of **vehicles** are necessary during a disaster because people and goods need to be moved from one place to another.

   a. innovative ideas

   b. machines used for transportation

   c. workers

9. It can be difficult to provide **relief** during a disaster. There are often many people who need different kinds of help, such as medical care and food.

   a. assistance

   b. comfort

   c. freedom

10. If you **overwhelm** the networks, they will eventually shut down and stop working.

    a. put too much pressure on

    b. spend too much time on

    c. work too hard on

E COMMUNICATE Use the scale below to indicate how strongly you agree or disagree with each of the statements below. Then with a partner, take turns explaining your answers. Use the words in bold in your answers.

1 = strongly disagree   2 = disagree   3 = agree   4 = strongly agree

A: *I agree with number 1. I am pretty **resilient**. For example, there was a bad fire in our house when I was 15 and we lost everything. It was difficult at first, but after a few months I felt OK again.*

B: *I really admire you for that. I gave myself a 1 for number 1. I don't think I'm very **resilient**. Even small things such as a having an argument with a friend upset me a lot.*

1. _____ I am very **resilient**.

2. _____ I believe that news programs should avoid all **imagery** of death and destruction.

3. _____ The **infrastructure** in the cities in my country is generally good.

4. _____ I don't care what kind of **vehicle** I drive, as long as it's safe and reliable.

5. _____ I can handle a lot of pressure. I am not easily **overwhelmed**.

6. _____ When I meet someone, I can usually trust my **initial** impression of him or her. I rarely change my opinion later.

7. _____ I would be good at helping with disaster **relief**.

WATCH

F ▶ **1.15** **WATCH FOR MAIN IDEAS** Watch the entire edited TED Talk. Check [✓] the two main ideas.

1. _____ Robots are essential in disaster relief because they significantly speed up the response to the disaster.

2. _____ Robots are important because they provide humans with the essential data that they need to respond quickly and efficiently to a disaster.

3. _____ Robots will one day replace human and animal disaster relief teams.

4. _____ Search and rescue robots are more effective at finding and rescuing people than human and animal disaster relief teams.

WORDS IN THE TALK

Cape Cod (n): an area of land in the state of Massachusetts, USA. Cape Cod is known for its great fishing sites.
claim (n): a demand for something that one has a right to
cognitive (adj): concerned with the act or process of knowing or thinking
hydrological (adj): relating to water
mitigate (v): to lessen; reduce the intensity or pain of something
resolution (n): focus on a camera

G ▶ **1.16** Watch the segments from the edited TED Talk. You will watch each segment two times. In your notebook, take notes about each main point. Include the most important details. Do *not* write down everything you hear.

Segment 1

Main Point: Disasters have a huge impact on the world.

Segment 2

Main Point: Why reducing response time is so important in a disaster

H Work with a partner. Look at your notes from exercise G. Did you write down the same things? Did you write down too much? If you did, cross something out. Did you miss something that you think is important? If so, add that information to your notes.

A helicopter lifts a victim after the March 2011 earthquake and tsunami, Watari Town, Northern Japan.

I **COMMUNICATE** Work with a new partner. Summarize the information included in your notes to explain the main ideas in exercise G. One student should summarize the information in Segment 1. The other student should summarize the information in Segment 2.

J ▶ **1.17** **WATCH FOR DETAILS** Read the information in Column B of the chart. Then watch the segment from the edited TED Talk. There will be some pauses. As you watch, match each of the topics in Column B with the correct type(s) of robot(s) in Column A. You will need to use some of the information from Column B more than once.

COLUMN A	COLUMN B
1. Hummingbird _____ **2.** Fixed Wing/Hawk _____ **3.** Sarbot Dolphin _____ **4.** Bujold _____	**a.** can go places people cannot go **b.** can fly **c.** can go underwater **d.** can go underground **e.** can take photos from all angles **f.** can take photos to make 3D models **g.** helped reopen a fishing port **h.** record data **i.** use sonar **j.** used at the WTC (World Trade Center) **k.** used in Oso mudslide

K **GIVE REASONS** Work with a partner. Take turns explaining how the four types of robots listed in exercise J are useful and the reasons why they are necessary.

L ▶ **1.18** **EXPAND YOUR VOCABULARY** Watch the excerpts from the TED Talk. Guess the meanings of the phrases in the box.

> pull (something) together   put at risk   the odds   sort (something) out
> wipe out   game changer   happen to (do/have something)

M **WATCH MORE** Go to TED.com to watch the full TED Talk by Robin Murphy.

AFTER YOU WATCH

N **THINK CRITICALLY** **Analyze.** Read Robin Murphy's idea worth spreading. Then discuss the questions in a small group.

> Robin Murphy's idea worth spreading is that robots can help us reduce the initial response time after a disaster, which will save lives and speed the community's recovery.

1. Although robots can be useful, some people worry about them. Why do you think they are worried? What would Murphy say to convince these people not to worry?

2. At the end of Robin Murphy's talk, she says, "So really, 'disaster robotics' is a misnomer (an incorrect name for something). It's not about the robots. It's about the data." Explain what she means.

Put It Together

A **THINK CRITICALLY** **Synthesize.** Work in a small group. Look at the list of capabilities in the chart. Based on what you have learned from the lecture in Part 1 and the edited TED Talk in Part 2, decide if animals, robots, or both have each capability, and put a check [✓] in the correct column(s). Do *not* put a check if the information was not mentioned in the lecture or edited TED Talk.

CAPABILITIES	ANIMALS	ROBOTS
1. find missing people		
2. find people who are buried		
3. prevent disasters		
4. can be controlled remotely (from a distance)		
5. save money		
6. give us a lot of data		
7. form relationships with people		
8. have excellent visual ability		
9. have an excellent sense of smell		

B **THINK CRITICALLY** **Apply.** Look at the chart in exercise A. Are there any capabilities that you know are true for animals or robots even though they were not mentioned specifically in the lecture or edited TED Talk? If yes, add an X in the appropriate column of the chart. Then share your knowledge with your group.

A raven flying in a forest in Alberta, Canada

COMMUNICATE

ASSIGNMENT: Participate in a Group Role Play You will participate in a group role play about robot designs. You will work in a group to design a robot. You will then present your robot design to your classmates. Your classmates will play the role of individual investors. They will each decide which group's robot to invest in. Review the ideas in Parts 1 and 2 and the listening and speaking skills as you prepare for your role play.

PREPARE

PRESENTATION SKILL **Use Body Language Effectively**

Body language—that is, eye contact and gestures—is very important when presenting. Eye contact helps you hold people's attention. Carefully selected gestures support your verbal (spoken) message. Watch the excerpt from the TED Talk, and notice how the speaker . . .

▶ 1.19

- uses eye contact to connect with the audience and appear confident.
- uses gestures to emphasize and illustrate her verbal message—but only uses gestures with a clear purpose.

(See page 173 of the *Independent Student Handbook* for more information on using body language.)

C ▶ **1.20** Read the transcript as you watch the excerpt from the TED Talk. Underline the words that Murphy emphasizes with her gestures. In addition, notice how she uses eye contact.

> The problem becomes: Who gets what data when? One thing to do is to ship all the information to everybody and let them sort it out. Well, the problem with that is it overwhelms the networks, and worse yet, it overwhelms the cognitive abilities of each of the people trying to get that one nugget of information they need to make the decision that's going to make the difference.

D **COMMUNICATE** Work with a partner. Compare the sections that you underlined in exercise C. Then discuss the effect that Murphy's body language had on you. Did it help you understand what she was saying? Did it help you concentrate? Did it make you more interested in what she was saying? Explain your answers.

A climbing robot with the structure and movement of a gecko

E **COLLABORATE** Work in a group. Prepare for the group role play. Follow these steps.

- Decide on a type of robot to present.

- Decide on the purpose of your robot. Consider what you have learned in the edited TED Talk, and discuss the following questions:

   o **Why** is your robot needed? **How** will it help people?

   o **What** will it be able to do? **How** will it work?

   o **Who** will use it and **when** and **where** will they use it (in what kinds of situations)?

- Draw a picture of your robot.

- Prepare a sales presentation to convince "investors" (your classmates) to invest in your robot. Use the questions above to guide your presentation. Assign a part of the presentation to each member of the group.

- Practice your presentation. Practice using body language, such as gestures and eye contact, to help emphasize important information and connect with your audience.

PRESENT

F Read the rubric on page 180. Notice how your presentation will be evaluated. Keep these categories in mind as you present and watch your classmates.

G Follow the instructions.

Robot Designers: Present your robot to the "investors" (your classmates). Remember that your goal is to convince them to invest in your robot.

Audience (Individual Investors): You have $10,000 to invest in one group's robot. You cannot invest in your own group's robot, and you must invest all of your money in one robot. Watch the other groups' presentations. Ask questions. After all of the groups have presented, make your decision on which robot you will invest in. Be ready to explain the reasons for your choice to the class.

H **THINK CRITICALLY Evaluate.** With your group, discuss the feedback you received. Discuss what your group did well and what might make your presentation even stronger.

REFLECT

Reflect on what you have learned. Check [✓] your progress.

I can
- [ ] ask questions while listening.
- [ ] give reasons to support my main points.
- [ ] use correct syllable stress.
- [ ] include only essential details in my notes.
- [ ] use body language effectively when presenting.

I understand the meanings of these words and can use them.
Circle those you know. Underline those you need to work on.

access AWL	initial AWL	resilient	structural AWL
activate	innovative AWL	responder	survivor AWL
devastated	overwhelm	restore AWL	vehicle AWL
imagery AWL	process AWL	sensor	wilderness
infrastructure AWL	relief	site AWL	underestimate AWL

Beyond Limits

IN ANY Thing
YOU do you
MUST Focus

When Kelvin Doe was 13 years old, he began searching through the trash cans of Freetown, Sierra Leone, looking for spare electronic parts. Eventually, he found enough parts to put together an entire homemade radio station. Now he broadcasts music, comedy, and news features to his community under the nickname General Focus.

THINK AND DISCUSS

1 Read the unit title. What do you think it means?

2 Look at the photo and read the caption. How do you think Kelvin Doe's story relates to the title? Explain your answers.

PART 1

Different Brains, Different
Ways of Learning

BEFORE YOU LISTEN

A COMMUNICATE Work in a small group. Discuss these questions.

1. Look at the photo and read the title of the radio interview, *Different Brains, Different Ways of Learning*. How do you think the photo relates to the title?

2. Read the definition of *autism* below. Based on the definition and your own knowledge, what are some of the challenges that people with autism and their families face? What types of extraordinary abilities do some people with autism have, other than mathematics?

> **Autism** is a complex developmental disorder. People with autism often have problems with social interaction and verbal and nonverbal communication. Some people with autism also have extraordinary ability in a specialized field such as mathematics. For example, they may be able to do rapid, complex mental calculations that usually only a computer can do.

Brain scan of Temple Grandin, left, compared to someone without autism. Grandin's visual output area is much larger than a typical person's.

B ☊ **1.27** **THINK CRITICALLY** Predict. Read the questions about the radio interview you are going to hear and predict the answers. Then listen to the beginning of the interview and check [✓] your answers.

1. Who do you think the host is going to interview?

_____ a doctor who studies autism

_____ a graduate student who studies the brain

_____ a person with autism

2. What topics do you think the radio show host and the guest are going to discuss?

_____ research on people with unusual brains

_____ the causes and treatment of autism

_____ the achievements of people with unusual brains

VOCABULARY

C ☊ **1.28** Read and listen to the sentences with words from the radio interview. Choose the meaning for each word.

1. We all have **limitations** that make it difficult for us to do certain things. For example, I do not have a good visual sense, so I would probably never be an artist.
   a. expectations **b.** restrictions in ability **c.** terrible problems

2. When the interviewer did not understand something that the interviewee said, she asked for **clarification**.
   a. an explanation **b.** extra time **c.** questions

3. She took her son to a doctor because of his unusual behavior. The doctor **diagnosed** him with autism, but unfortunately, at the time, there was nothing the doctor could suggest to help the child.
   a. treated **b.** carefully examined **c.** identified (a medical condition)

4. Some brain conditions stay the same; others get **progressively** worse over time.
   a. frequently **b.** increasingly **c.** rarely

5. Teachers do not always know how students are going to do on tests. Some good students have poorer **outcomes** than their teachers expect.
   a. reasons **b.** behavior **c.** results

6. When the dancer injured his leg, everyone thought the injury would mean the **destruction** of his career. However, he recovered and was stronger than ever.
   a. act of forgetting something **b.** method of change **c.** process of destroying

7. Because of her brain injury, she has difficulty with hand-eye **coordination**. She cannot move her hands quickly enough to respond to something she sees. For example, she cannot catch a ball.

   a. ability to communicate   **b.** ability to move the body well   **c.** ability to see

8. Some animals become **paralyzed** with fear and don't move when they are frightened; others run away or attack.

   a. angry   **b.** easy to handle   **c.** unable to move

9. We all pay attention to different things. Something that is easily **visible** to one person might not be noticed by another person.

   a. able to be seen   **b.** colored   **c.** understood

10. Traveling to other countries can **transform** your ideas about the world. When you travel, you have the opportunity to learn about different places, people, and cultures.

   a. make a big change in   **b.** transfer   **c.** keep the same

D **COMMUNICATE** Circle the affirmative or negative form to make each sentence true for you. Then explain your answers to a partner. Use the words in bold.

> A: *Learning English has definitely **transformed** my way of thinking. Sometimes I feel like a different person when I'm speaking English!*
>
> B: *Really? I don't think it has **transformed** my way of thinking, but I do think it has opened up new opportunities for my future.*

1. Learning another language has **transformed** / hasn't **transformed** my way of thinking.

2. With hard work, it is/isn't possible to overcome most of the **limitations** in your life.

3. When I have a lot of choices, I feel/don't feel **paralyzed**. It is/isn't difficult for me to make a decision.

4. When I am talking to a native speaker and I don't understand something, I feel/don't feel comfortable asking for **clarification**.

5. As we get older, it becomes/doesn't become **progressively** more difficult to change our habits.

6. Hard work is/is not always necessary for a good **outcome** in school.

LISTEN

E 🎧 **1.29 LISTEN FOR MAIN IDEAS** Read the statements. Then listen to the interview. For each statement, write T for *true*, F for *false*, or N for items *not mentioned* in the interview.

1. _____ Most of the people in Sarah's study are autistic.

2. _____ One of Dr. Grandin's strengths is her ability to think and learn visually.

3. _____ Another one of Dr. Grandin's strengths is her short-term memory.

4. _____ Dr. Grandin probably sees herself as someone who is successful in spite of her unusual brain.

5. _____ Dr. Grandin's career is perfect for her because of the way she thinks and learns.

6. _____ Dr. Grandin wants people to realize that autism is a serious disability.

WORDS IN THE INTERVIEW

abstract (adj): not a concrete reality, a specific object, or an actual example
an institution (n): a place where people who can't take care of themselves live

Dr. Temple Grandin with cows

F **LISTEN FOR DETAILS** Listen and fill in the missing words for each segment. Then answer the questions that follow.

🎧 **1.31** Segment 1

Well, Dr. Grandin is highly intelligent, as her achievements show. However, she still finds many everyday things ___dificul___ (1) or impossible to do. For example, she is unable to remember more than three simple instructions, and she has extreme ___dificul___ (2) with abstract thinking. These ___dificulties___ (3) could have meant the destruction of her dream of becoming a scientist.

1. What word is repeated? ___dificul___

2. What is the key point of this segment? _____

🎧 **1.32** Segment 2

Her family's support was important, but scans of Dr. Grandin's ___brain___ (1) also provide some answers. The part of her ___brain___ (2) that controls the coordination of movement is 20 percent smaller than average. The area that ___handel___ (3) short-term memory is also small. On the other hand, the side that ___proces___ (4) visual information is unusually large. This helps explain her effective approach to thinking and learning.

1. Which word is repeated? _____

2. What words are synonyms? _____ and _____

3. What is the key point of this segment? _____

AFTER YOU LISTEN

G THINK CRITICALLY Reflect. Work in a small group. Discuss and answer the questions.

1. Considering what you have learned from the radio interview and the life of Dr. Temple Grandin, what are some careers that people with autism might be particularly good at? Check [✓] the careers below and add some of your own ideas.

   _____ graphic artist _____ journalist _____ teacher _____ radio host

   _____ computer programmer _____ veterinarian _____ doctor

   Your ideas: _____ , _____

2. In the radio interview, Sarah says that many of the people in the study believe that their success is *because of* their differences and limitations, rather than *in spite of* them. What is the difference in meaning between *because of* and *in spite of*? Do you agree that being different can lead to success? Explain your answer with examples.

H COMMUNICATE Share and discuss your ideas from exercise G with the class.

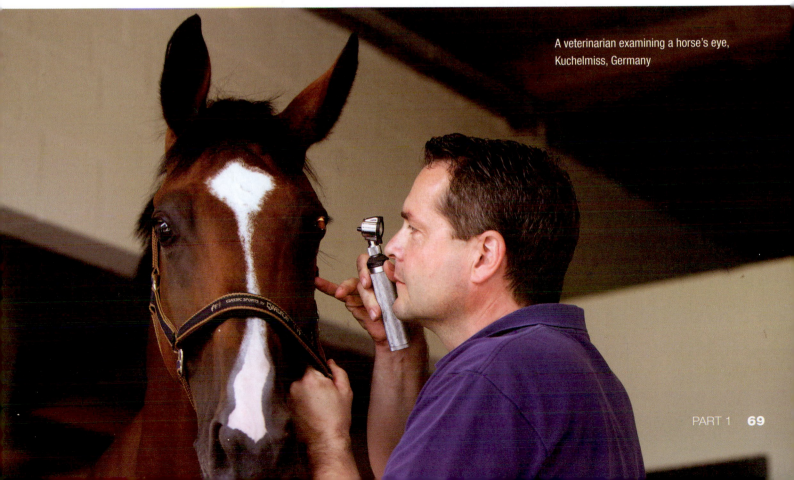

A veterinarian examining a horse's eye, Kuchelmiss, Germany

SPEAKING

I 🎧 **1.35** Listen to the words. Check [✓] the ending you hear for each word. Then listen again and repeat each word after the speaker.

	[d]	[t]	[əd]
1. asked	___	___	___
2. identified	___	___	___
3. happened	___	___	___
4. paralyzed	___	___	___
5. diagnosed	___	___	___
6. transformed	___	___	___
7. expected	___	___	___
8. covered	___	___	___
9. contacted	___	___	___
10. developed	___	___	___

J 🎧 **1.36** Listen to the excerpt from the radio interview. Using the boldfaced signal words and phrases as reference points, complete the notes with the most important information from the story. Don't write full sentences. Use abbreviations of key words.

One time _____ prblm in cattl facil _____

when suddenly _____ always same plc, but nb knew why ____

It was then that _____

As soon as _____

_____

Once _____

K **COMMUNICATE** Work with a partner. Take turns retelling the story from exercise J. Use the signal words and phrases as you tell the story. Pay attention to the pronunciation of *–ed* endings.

A cattle corral and chute system designed by Temple Grandin

L **THINK CRITICALLY** **Analyze.** Work in a group. Look at the figure of the brain and discuss the questions below.

PARTS OF THE BRAIN

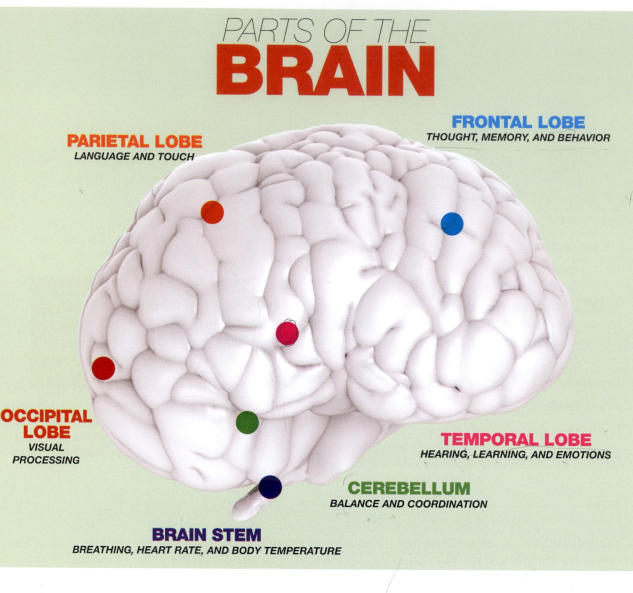

FRONTAL LOBE
THOUGHT, MEMORY, AND BEHAVIOR

PARIETAL LOBE
LANGUAGE AND TOUCH

OCCIPITAL LOBE
VISUAL PROCESSING

TEMPORAL LOBE
HEARING, LEARNING, AND EMOTIONS

CEREBELLUM
BALANCE AND COORDINATION

BRAIN STEM
BREATHING, HEART RATE, AND BODY TEMPERATURE

1. Which area of the brain is responsible for coordination? For memory?

2. Which functions is the parietal lobe responsible for?

3. Which area of the brain do you think is most important? Why?

4. Which areas of Temple Grandin's brain are probably more developed than those of someone with a "typical" brain? Why?

5. Which areas do you think are probably the most developed in a professional soccer player's brain? Why?

6. Which areas so you think are probably the most developed in an artist's brain? Why?

7. Think of activities that you are able and unable to do well. Which areas of your brain do you think are the most developed? Least developed? Why?

PART 2

TEDTALKS

Embrace the shake

❝ . . . we need to first be limited in order to become limitless. **❞**

BEFORE YOU WATCH

A **COMMUNICATE** Work with a partner. Read the title. The word *embrace* has two meanings:

1. hold someone in your arms (usually with love or affection)

2. accept or support something enthusiastically

Now read the information about the TED speaker. Which of the two meanings do you think is used in the title? What is a *shake*? What do you think the title means?

PHIL HANSEN   Multimedia Artist

When Phil Hansen was attending art school, he developed a very bad shake in his hand, which made it impossible for him to draw. He quit art school, stopped making art, and, for a time, lost his way in life. However, Hansen finally visited a doctor about his condition. The doctor asked him a question that would change his life, "Why not embrace the shake?"

Since then, Hansen has returned to a career in art and has devoted himself to teaching new ways of looking at creativity. Hansen is now a well-known artist who produces highly unusual pieces of art.

An example of pointillism by Phil Hansen

B **THINK CRITICALLY** Predict. Hansen repeats each of the words below several times during his talk. Based on these words and the information about him on page 73, what do you think the talk is going to be about? Discuss your ideas with a partner.

> art/artistic   create/creation/creativity   limit/limitation   shake   destroy/destruction   image

C **COMMUNICATE** Work in a small group. Ask and answer these questions.

1. What do you think might be difficult about being an artist? Do you know any artists? If so, tell your group about them.

2. What is a *limitation?* What kinds of limitations could make it difficult for someone to become an artist?

3. Have you or someone else you know ever wanted to do something but couldn't do it because of some kind of limitation? If so, tell your group about it. The limitation could be physical, mental, financial, personal, or something else.

VOCABULARY

D 🎧 **1.37** Read and listen to the quotes and rephrased information from the edited TED Talk. Guess the meanings of the words in bold. Write T for *true* or F for *false* for each statement that follows. Then change the false statements to make them true.

1. After many years of drawing, Hansen developed a shake in his hand. When his hand shook, he tried to **compensate** by holding the pen more tightly. This didn't help. In fact, it made things worse.

   _____ When you **compensate** for something that you can't do or are not very good at doing, you try to fix the problem by doing something in a different way.

2. The shake in Hansen's hand was so bad that he couldn't draw a straight line. **Ultimately**, he had to find new ways to make art.

   _____ **Ultimately** means at first, in the beginning.

3. "And more importantly, once I embraced the shake, I realized I could still make art. I just had to find a different **approach** to making the art that I wanted."

   _____ When we find a different **approach** to something, we find a different way of handling it.

4. In his art, Hansen likes to **fragment** images. When you look at the image up close, you see individual dots of ink. But when you look at the image from farther away, you see that the dots make up an entire image, for example, a face.

   _____ When you **fragment** something, you break it up into small pieces.

5. "This was the first time I'd **encountered** this idea that embracing a limitation could actually drive creativity."

   _____ When you **encounter** an idea, you experience or hear about it.

6. He didn't even have the basic things that most artists have to work with, so when he got a job and his first paycheck, he was excited to finally be able to buy the **supplies** he needed.

   _____ Some examples of art **supplies** are clothing and food.

7. "And I was in a dark place for a long time, unable to create. And it didn't make any sense, because I was finally able to support my art, and yet I was creatively **blank**."

   _____ When you feel **blank**, you have no ideas. Your mind is empty.

8. "Or what if instead of making art to **display**, I had to destroy it?"

   _____ When you **display** your art, you usually destroy it.

9. To an artist, creativity is an important **resource**.

   _____ A **resource** is something that is both available for you and helpful to you.

10. "Learning to be creative within the confines of our limitations is the best hope we have to transform ourselves and, **collectively**, transform our world."

    _____ When we do things **collectively**, we are usually working alone.

E **COMMUNICATE** Work with a partner. Read and answer the questions. Use the vocabulary in bold in your answers.

> A: *Some people* **compensate** *for losing their eyesight by getting Seeing Eye dogs.*
>
> B: *True. Also, when people lose one of their senses, their other senses often become stronger to help* **compensate**.

1. What are some ways that people can **compensate** for losing their eyesight? Going deaf? Having a broken arm? (If you are not sure, just imagine what they might have done.)

2. What types of **supplies** does a painter need? A sculptor? A photographer?

3. Does your mind ever go **blank** when you are taking a test? In what other types of situations do people's minds tend to go **blank**?

4. What are some of the places where artists can **display** their artwork? What are some of the most unusual places where you have seen artwork **displayed**?

5. What types of **resources** does someone need to become a great artist? To learn a foreign language? To start a business?

6. Do you believe that great discoveries and achievements are more often made individually or **collectively**? You can talk about discoveries in art, science, or any other field you are interested in.

learnmore The expression "think outside the box" is frequently used in English. It began appearing in the business community in the 1960s and 1970s to encourage employees to look for solutions outside their usual ways of thinking. The expression is now widely used in all fields to express the idea that we should not feel limited by what already exists, but should be looking for new ideas or new approaches to old ideas.

Judy Samakie, Mohanad Ghashim (on the slide), and Hussam Ali Kaj at the offices of Oasis 500

WATCH

F ▶ **1.21** **WATCH FOR MAIN IDEAS** Watch the edited TED Talk. Check [✓] the sentences that Phil Hansen would probably agree with.

1. _____ Everyone has limitations.

2. _____ Individual limitations can be opportunities to find creative solutions.

3. _____ Having the complete freedom to do whatever you want to do can be paralyzing.

4. _____ To be successful, an artist should have some kind of physical limitation.

G ▶ **1.21** **WATCH FOR DETAILS** Read the important events in Hansen's life below. Then watch the edited TED Talk again and number the events in the correct order. Write *1* next to the first event, *2* next to the second event, and so on.

a. _____ He realized he could use his limitation as a source of creativity and began to create art in new ways.

b. _____ He got a job and was excited to be able to buy lots of art supplies, but he felt paralyzed by all of his choices.

c. _____ He decided to become even more creative by placing more limitations on himself.

d. _____ He damaged his hand and developed a shake.

e. _____ He decided to follow the doctor's advice to "embrace the shake."

f. _____ He finally went to see a doctor.

g. _____ He quit art school and stopped making art.

NOTE-TAKING SKILL **Write Key Words and Phrases**

If a word or phrase is repeated in a listening, it is probably important, so you should include it in your notes. Use the same abbreviation for all forms of a repeated word or phrase.

Example: difficult/difficulty > *diffclt*
ultimate/ultimately > *ultmt*

H Write abbreviations for the repeated words from the edited TED Talk.

1. artistic _____

2. create/creations/creativity

_____

3. limit/limitation _____

4. destroy/destruction _____

5. image _____

6. approach _____

I ▶ **1.22** **WATCH AND TAKE NOTES** Watch the segments from the edited TED Talk. In your notebook, take notes to answer the questions for each segment. Use your abbreviations from exercise H where appropriate. Do not write full sentences.

Segment 1: Hansen's Hand

1. What happened to his hand?

2. Why/How did it happen?

3. What was the result?

Segment 2: The First Change in Hansen's Approach to Creating Art

4. Why did he change his approach to creating art?

5. How did he change his approach?

6. What are some examples of the new art he created with this approach?

Segment 3: The Second Change in Hansen's Approach to Creating Art

7. What made him change his approach to creating art again?

8. What are some examples of the new art he created with the new approach?

J **EXPLAIN A SEQUENCE OF EVENTS** With a partner, take turns telling the events in Hansen's life, using your notes from exercise I to help you.

- Use at least two signal words or phrases from the Speaking Skill box on page 70 to show the sequence of events.
- Pay attention to the pronunciation of *–ed* endings.

K ▶ **1.23** **EXPAND YOUR VOCABULARY** Watch the excerpts from the TED Talk. Guess the meanings of each phrase.

go nuts	come up with	let go
came to mind	go through the motions	

L **WATCH MORE** Go to TED.com to watch the full TED Talk by Phil Hansen.

AFTER YOU WATCH

M **COLLABORATE** Work with a partner. Read Phil Hansen's idea worth spreading. Then complete the activities that follow.

> Phil Hansen's idea worth spreading is that when we creatively embrace our limitations, we can discover new possibilities.

1. Write Hansen's *idea worth spreading* using your own words. Then share your version with the class. As a class, decide whose version is best.

2. Think about the examples of Hansen's art work that you saw in the edited TED Talk. Discuss your own opinion of his work.

Put It Together

A THINK CRITICALLY Synthesize. Work in a group. Check [✓] the statements that you think both Temple Grandin and Phil Hansen would agree with. Then explain your answers by referring to the radio interview in Part 1 and the TED Talk in Part 2.

1. _____ We should work hard to overcome the difficulties in our lives.

2. _____ All people have limitations and must learn to work with those limitations.

3. _____ Accepting your limitations frees you to become more creative and productive.

4. _____ Our individual challenges can be very difficult to accept.

5. _____ A difference is not a disability.

COMMUNICATE

ASSIGNMENT: Give an Individual Presentation You are going to prepare a presentation on someone who had a limitation and overcame it or used it in order to become successful in some way. Review the ideas in Parts 1 and 2 and the listening and speaking skills as you prepare your presentation.

PREPARE

PRESENTATION SKILL Use Repetition and Rephrasing

When a presenter repeats key words, it can make the presentation easier to follow. It also helps the audience focus on and remember the presenter's main ideas. Read and watch the example from the talk.

▶ 1.24

As I destroyed each project, I was learning to let go, let go of outcomes, let go of failures, and let go of imperfections. And in return, I found a process of creating art that's perpetual and unencumbered by results.

The repetition of the phrase *let go* shows you that this is an important point for the speaker.

(For more information on repetition and rephrasing, see page 165 of the *Independent Student Handbook.*)

B Choose the person you are going to talk about in your presentation. Then complete the outline. Do not write full sentences. Depending on who you choose to talk about, you might need to add, change, or eliminate a question in the outline.

I.   Beginning

    A. Who is this person? (Name and relationship to you, for example, a famous person, coworker, family member, friend, etc.)

          _____

    B. Where is he or she from? _____

    C. What other background information is important to know about this person?

          _____

    D. What is his or her limitation?

          _____

II.   Middle

    A. When and how did this limitation begin?

          _____

    B. What difficulties did he or she face because of the limitation?

          _____

    C. What did he or she do to make use of the limitation?

          _____

III.   End

    A. What can we learn from this person?

          _____

C Prepare for your presentation. Follow these steps.

- Review the information in the Speaking Skill box on page 70. Write signal words or phrases in the appropriate parts of your outline to show the sequence of events.

- Decide which key words you should repeat and which ideas you should state and then rephrase. Write them in the appropriate places in your outline.

- Take the information from your outline and write it on note cards. Do *not* write full sentences on your note cards. Just write the words and phrases that will help you remember the important points of your presentation. Circle those that you will repeat. Also write the signal words and phrases you will use.

Mordecai "Three Finger" Brown pitching a baseball. Mordecai Brown's damaged hand enabled him to throw pitches that were very difficult for batters to hit.

I. Beginning
- Mordecai Brown (1876-1948)
- Famous (baseball) (player) (a pitcher); nickname "Three Finger Brown"
- from Nyesville, Indiana, USA
- had (damaged) (hand)

D Read the rubric on page 180. Notice how your presentation will be evaluated. Keep these categories in mind as you present and watch your classmates' presentations.

PRESENT

E Give your presentation to the class. Watch your classmates' presentations. After you watch each one, provide feedback using the rubric as a guide. Add notes or any other feedback you want to share.

F **THINK CRITICALLY Evaluate.** In a small group, discuss the feedback you received. Discuss what you did well and what might make your presentation even stronger.

REFLECT

Reflect on what you have learned. Check [✓] your progress.

I can
- ☐ recognize repetition and rephrasing of important words and ideas.
- ☐ explain a sequence of events using repetition and rephrasing to emphasize and clarify key ideas.
- ☐ use signal words and phrases appropriately when explaining a sequence of events.
- ☐ pronounce –ed on the ends of words correctly.
- ☐ take notes by writing key words and phrases.

I understand the meanings of these words and can use them.
Circle those you know. Underline those you need to work on.

approach AWL	coordination AWL	fragment AWL	resources AWL
blank	destruction	limitation	supplies
clarification AWL	diagnose	outcome AWL	transform AWL
collectively AWL	display AWL	paralyzed	ultimately AWL
compensate AWL	encounter AWL	progressively	visible

Stress: Friend or Foe?

Performers wait backstage at the Hungry Ghost Festival, Hong Kong(China). Stress can have a negative or positive effect on performance.

THINK AND DISCUSS

1 Read the unit title. What do you think *foe* means? What do you think this unit might be about?

2 Look at the photo. How do you think it relates to the title?

PART 1 How Stress Affects the Body

BEFORE YOU LISTEN

A **COMMUNICATE** Work in a small group. Discuss these questions.

1. Look at the picture. How do you think it relates to the title of the lecture, *How Stress Affects the Body*?

2. What kinds of stress do people face today? How is the stress we face today different from the stress our ancestors faced thousands of years ago?

B **THINK CRITICALLY** **Predict.** Work in a small group. Discuss these questions and predict the answers that you will hear in the lecture.

1. Is stress good, bad, or neutral (neither good nor bad) for our overall physical and mental health? Explain your answer.

2. Are you familiar with the expression "fight or flight"? If so, how does it relate to stress? If not, listen carefully to how the lecturer explains it.

3. What effect does stress have on the heart?

Early humans hunting a mammoth

VOCABULARY

C 🎧 **2.2** Read and listen to the sentences with words and phrases from the lecture. Guess the meaning of each bold word or phrase. Then write each word or phrase next to its definition.

a. Most people get headaches from time to time, but if you suffer from **chronic** headaches, you should probably see a doctor. It is not normal to have a headache every day.

b. Having a baby is stressful both emotionally and physically. Fortunately, there is a **mechanism** in women's bodies to help them deal with the stress. After the baby is born, the mother's brain **releases** a hormone called oxytocin. Oxytocin **strengthens** the new mother's emotional connection to her baby so that she will be more likely to keep the baby safe.

c. Firefighters have stressful jobs. They have to face danger and remain calm. They must learn to control their emotions in a **crisis**.

d. If you eat too much and never walk anywhere or exercise your **muscles**, your body will **inevitably** become weak and you will gain weight. There is no other possibility.

e. Research has **revealed** that stress can **be associated with** serious health problems. For example, people under a lot of stress are more likely to have higher blood pressure and more heart attacks than people with less stress. Stress can also cause depression. To **enhance** your quality of life, you should learn healthy ways to manage stress.

1. _____ (n) a system with a specific purpose or way of doing something

2. _____ (adv) unavoidably

3. _____ (v phrase) be closely connected to

4. _____ (v) puts or sends out (into the body)

5. _____ (v) makes stronger

6. _____ (v) uncovered; shown

7. _____ (v) improve; add to

8. _____ (n) an emergency

9. _____ (n) tissues connected to the bones that make the body move

10. _____ (adj) continuing for a long time

A woman with her two-year-old boy kayaks down a flooded street in Hampton, Virginia, USA after a storm on the Chesapeake Bay.

D **COMMUNICATE** Choose the affirmative or negative form in each sentence to make it true for you. Then explain your answers to a partner.

> A: *In a **crisis**, I'm usually able to remain calm and think clearly. I think it's because I'm the oldest of five kids, and there was always some kind of **crisis** happening!*
>
> B: *Really? I'm useless in a **crisis**. I freeze and my mind goes blank.*

1. In a **crisis,** I <u>am / am not</u> usually able to remain calm and think clearly.

2. I <u>believe / don't believe</u> that eating a healthy diet **enhances** your ability to deal with stress.

3. I <u>need / don't need</u> to **strengthen** my ability to deal with stress in my life.

4. I <u>**reveal** / don't **reveal**</u> my emotions to people that I don't know very well.

5. In my opinion, most psychological problems <u>are / are not</u> **associated with** the stresses of modern life.

6. I <u>believe / don't believe</u> that it is more effective to **release** negative feelings through physical activity than by talking.

LISTEN

E 🎧 **2.3** ▶ **1.25** **LISTEN FOR MAIN IDEAS** Read the sentences and answer choices. Then listen to the lecture and choose the correct answers.

1. Stress is _____.
   a. almost always harmful to our health
   b. harmful to our health when it lasts for a short time
   c. important for our survival in a crisis

2. Acute stress _____ .

    a. is dangerous over the short term

    b. does not last for a long time

    c. is often harmful to our health

3. "Fight or flight" refers to _____ .

    a. the body's natural reaction to danger

    b. the dangerous effects of stress on the body

    c. the release of hormones from the brain, which makes us want to fight

4. Chronic stress _____ .

    a. can last for a short or long period of time

    b. can make us sick because it lasts for a long time

    c. does not last for very long but is very harmful

5. When compared to our ancestors thousands of years ago, today we experience _____ .

    a. more acute stress because life is more dangerous than ever before

    b. more chronic stress because psychological fears last longer than physical danger

    c. more acute and chronic stress because we are in more physical danger

---

LISTENING SKILL   **Listen for Cause and Effect**

When you listen to a lecture, it is important to understand cause-and-effect relationships. Sometimes you need to infer the relationship from the context; other times the speaker will use signal words and phrases.

🎧 **2.4** Read and listen to the examples from the lecture.

as a result (introductory adverb)

> *As a result, your blood pressure and breathing rate remain high and your muscles don't relax.*

be caused by (verb)

> *Nowadays, our stress tends to be caused by psychological fear or worry about the future, not physical danger.*

lead to (verb)

> *This leads to chronic stress. . . .*

affect (verb)

> *Next week we will talk about how chronic stress can affect the brain, the stomach, and the muscles.*

effect (noun)

> *The effects of chronic stress on the heart are the easiest to explain.*

WORDS IN THE LECTURE

hormone (n): a chemical from body organs that stimulates activity in living systems

F 🎧 **2.5** **LISTEN FOR DETAILS** Listen to segments of the lecture. Complete the flow charts to show the cause-and-effect relationships.

Segment 1

ACUTE STRESS

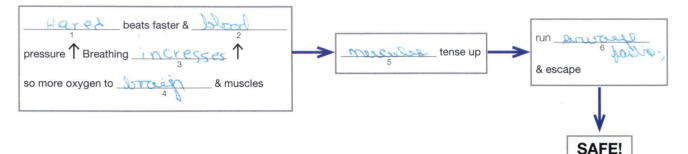

Hared beats faster & _blood_ pressure ↑ Breathing _increses_ ↑ so more oxygen to _brain_ & muscles

mescules tense up

run _aroself fastro_ & escape

SAFE!

Segment 2

CHRONIC STRESS

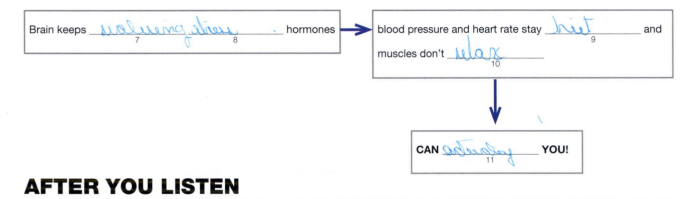

Brain keeps _noluuency stress_. hormones

blood pressure and heart rate stay _hiet_ and muscles don't _relax_

CAN _overwelm_ YOU!

AFTER YOU LISTEN

G THINK CRITICALLY Apply. Work in a small group. Discuss these questions.

1. The lecturer states that psychological fears are more likely to cause chronic stress than actual physical danger. In the modern world, are the following more likely to be psychological fears or real physical dangers? Write P (for *psychological* fear) or D (for physical *danger*). Explain your answers.

_____ getting bad grades

_____ falling from a great height, such as the top of a tall building or bridge

_____ giving a speech/speaking in front of an audience

_____ the dark

_____ spiders

_____ getting into a car accident

_____ snakes

_____ losing your cell phone

_____ someone breaking into your home

2. Which of the things in question 1 cause you stress? What other things in your life cause you stress? Are they physical dangers or psychological fears?

3. What are some things that you do to deal with stress?

A funnel spider in its web, Yerevan, Armenia

SPEAKING

SPEAKING SKILL Talk about Cause and Effect

When talking about cause and effect, signal words are useful, but you need to use them correctly. Study the information in the chart. Pay attention to whether the words are nouns or verbs, the word order, and the prepositions (if any).

VERB	NOUN
affect *Chronic stress **affects** the body in many ways.*	**effect (of) . . . (on) . . .** *An **effect of** chronic stress **on** the body is an increased risk of heart disease.*
cause *Chronic stress can **cause** headaches.*	**cause (of)** *Chronic stress can be the **cause of** headaches.*
result (in) *A stress response that lasts too long **results in** chronic stress.*	**result (of)** *Chronic stress is the **result of** a stress response that lasts too long.*

(See page 164 of the *Independent Student Handbook* for more information on talking about cause and effect.)

H **COMMUNICATE** Rewrite the questions using the noun form or verb form of the words in bold. Then with a partner, take turns asking and answering the questions with ideas from the lecture and your own ideas.

1. What are the **causes** of chronic stress? What _____?

2. What does too much stress **result** in? What are the _____?

3. How does stress **affect** your everyday life? What are the _____?

I **COMMUNICATE** Work with a partner. Look at the flow charts in exercise F on page 88. Student A will explain the flow chart on acute stress. Student B will explain the flow chart on chronic stress. Explain the causes and effects with the words and expressions from the Speaking Skill and Listening Skill boxes.

J **THINK CRITICALLY** **Interpret an Infographic.** Look at the infographic on stress. Work in a small group and answer the questions on page 91.

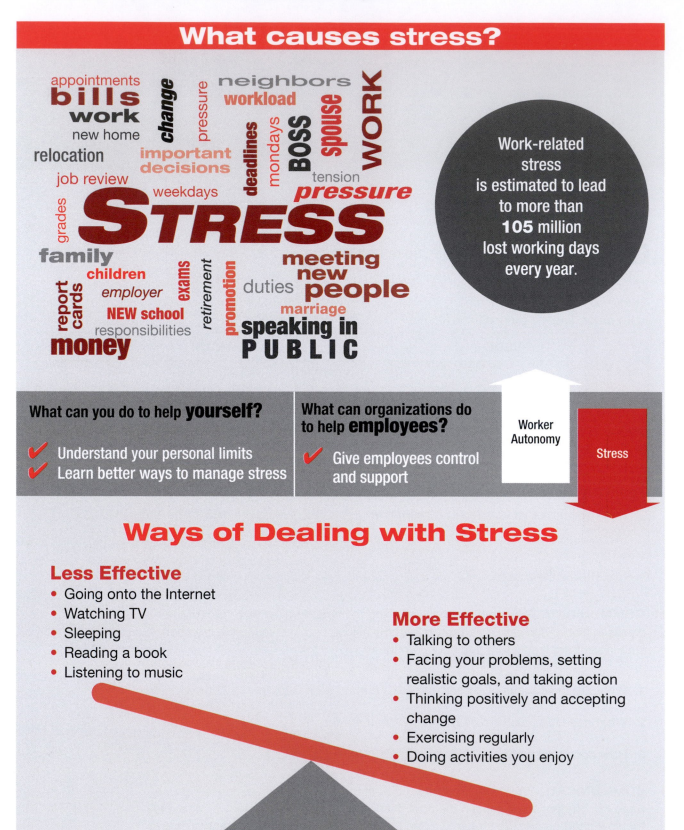

What causes stress?

appointments
bills
work
new home
relocation
job review
change
neighbors
workload
pressure
deadlines
mondays
BOSS
spouse
WORK
important decisions
weekdays
tension
pressure
grades

STRESS

family
children
exams
retirement
promotion
duties
employer
NEW school
responsibilities
meeting new people
marriage
report cards
speaking in PUBLIC
money

Work-related stress is estimated to lead to more than **105** million lost working days every year.

What can you do to help yourself?

✔ Understand your personal limits
✔ Learn better ways to manage stress

What can organizations do to help employees?

✔ Give employees control and support

Worker Autonomy

Stress

Ways of Dealing with Stress

Less Effective
- Going onto the Internet
- Watching TV
- Sleeping
- Reading a book
- Listening to music

More Effective
- Talking to others
- Facing your problems, setting realistic goals, and taking action
- Thinking positively and accepting change
- Exercising regularly
- Doing activities you enjoy

Source: OPP Ltd.

1. Who do you think this infographic was designed for? Support your answer by referring to specific sections.

2. Look at the topics in the section titled "What causes stress?" Which three topics in this section cause you the most stress? Circle them. Then compare and discuss your answer with your group.

3. With your group, add three more topics to the the section titled "What causes stress?" Then share your topics with your classmates.

4. Which of the questions from the list below does the infographic answer? Check [✓] them. Then answer them.

   a. _____ What can people do to deal with stress?

   b. _____ How can employers create a better work environment for their workers?

   c. _____ Which is more effective in dealing with stress, talking to someone or listening to music alone?

   d. _____ Why does a feeling of control make someone feel less stressed out?

   e. _____ Why is exercising a better way to deal with stress than reading?

5. According to the infographic, who would be least likely to suffer from stress? Why?
   a. An administrative assistant who works 35 hours a week for a large company. He has two managers.
   b. The manager of a small travel agency. She works in the office 40 hours a week for three weeks a month. She spends the other week on business trips arranged by the owner of the company.
   c. The operations manager of a large software company. She works from 60 to 80 hours per week, sets her own schedule, and often works from home.

6. Is there anything in the infographic that you disagree with or do not understand? Discuss with your group.

7. Look at the section titled "Ways of Dealing with Stress" in the infographic. Which ones do you use? Which ones don't you use? Which ones do you think you might try to use in the future?

A stockbroker suffering from stress at work

PRONUNCIATION SKILL   Thought Groups

English speakers group words into segments of meaning called *thought groups*. Thought groups help the listener understand and process information. There is a small break or pause at the end of each thought group. Long sentences might contain several thought groups. Short sentences might contain just one or two.

🎧 **2.6** Read and listen to the example from the lecture.

You experience acute stress / when you are in physical danger. /

Acute stress / lasts only a short time, / just until the danger is gone. /

Although there are no definite rules for putting words into thought groups, here are some guidelines of phrases you should NOT separate:

- adjectives from the nouns they modify
  acute stress

- adverbs from the words they modify
  just until

- prepositions from the nouns or noun phrases that follow them
  in physical danger

- the parts of a verb (verb *be* and main verb)
  is gone

K 🎧 **2.7** Listen to the sentences from the lecture. Put a slash [/] at the end of each thought group.

1. *For example, imagine you're walking home when a big scary dog jumps out at you. What happens?*

2. *You are suddenly full of energy, ready to run away or fight. This is called the "fight or flight" reaction.*

3. *Where does all that energy come from? It starts with your brain releasing the powerful hormones adrenaline and cortisol.*

L 🎧 **2.7** Listen again and check your answers. Then with a partner, take turns reading the sentences according to your markings.

How to make stress your friend

❝ . . . I have changed my mind about stress, and today, I want to change yours. ❞

ED

BEFORE YOU WATCH

A **THINK CRITICALLY** **Predict.** Read the title and the information about the TED speaker. How do you think the TED Talk will be different from the lecture in Part 1, *The Effects of Stress on the Body*? How will it be similar? Discuss your ideas with a partner.

KELLY MCGONIGAL Psychologist

Stanford University psychologist Kelly McGonigal is a leader in the growing field of "science-help." Through books, articles, courses, and workshops, McGonigal works to help us understand and put into practice the latest scientific findings in psychology, neuroscience, and medicine.

McGonigal holds positions in both the Stanford Graduate School of Business and the School of Medicine. She is the author of a book titled *The Upside of Stress: Why Stress Is Good for You, and How to Get Good at It.*

B THINK CRITICALLY Predict. Check [✓] the information that you think the TED Talk will include. Then with a partner, compare and discuss your answers.

1. _____ positive effects of acute stress

2. _____ negative effects of chronic stress

3. _____ positive effects of chronic stress

4. _____ how we can control stress with medication

5. _____ how we can manage stress with relaxation and meditation

6. _____ how we can understand the causes of stress

VOCABULARY

C 🎧 **2.8** These sentences will help you understand words and phrases in the edited TED Talk. Read and listen to the sentences. Then choose the correct meaning or explanation for each word or phrase.

1. Keeping a secret can be very stressful. For years I didn't tell my wife that I had lost money in a bad business deal. As soon as I made a **confession** about what I had done, I felt so much better.
   When you make a **confession**, you _____.
   a. admit that you did something wrong   **b.** blame someone else   **c.** tell a lie

2. You need to take care of yourself. If you **are** not **willing to** reduce your stress levels, eat a healthy diet, and exercise every day, you will never get better. To **heal,** your body needs all of these things.
   If you **are willing to** do something, you _____.
   a. agree to do it   **b.** are excited about it   **c.** don't want to do it
   Heal means _____.
   a. become healthy again   **b.** grow up   **c.** take care

3. Teaching can be stressful, but it can also be rewarding. When students are successful, it **motivates** the teacher. Their success makes the teacher want to work even harder.
   Motivate means _____.
   a. to be successful at something   **b.** to give (someone) a reason to do something   **c.** to work hard at something

4. She is a great doctor. She cares deeply about her patients and is always very **compassionate**. In turn, her patients show their **appreciation** by sending her thank-you cards.
   Compassionate people _____.
   a. have a lot of experience   **b.** show sympathy for others   **c.** think deeply
   Appreciation means _____.
   a. kindness   **b.** thankfulness   **c.** understanding

Police officers before a crowd
in Washington, DC, USA

5. It takes **courage** to be a good police officer. The police have to face danger
every day and remain strong and calm. Good police officers also need to have
empathy. They need to be able to understand all different types of people and
their problems—even people who are very different from them. Finally, good
police officers need **resilience.** They need to be able to face stressful situations
day after day and stay strong, both emotionally and physically.

Courage means _____ .

a. bravery   b. kindness   c. understanding

Empathy means _____ .

a. knowledge about many things   b. the ability to understand other people's feelings   c. the need for help from someone else

Resilience is _____ .

a. emotional support and understanding   b. physical strength   c. the ability to recover from difficulty

6. After my best friend lost his job, I had to ask him how he was dealing with the
stress of being unemployed. I did not have **access** to his mind to know his
thoughts and feelings.
Access is the ability to _____ .

a. believe   b. go inside   c. think

D **COMMUNICATE** Work with a partner. Read and answer the questions. Use the
words in bold in your answers.

1. What or who **motivates** you to study hard? Why?

2. Who is the most **compassionate** person you know? What **compassionate**
things has he or she done?

3. What jobs require **empathy?** Explain your answer.

4. Who do you know that has a lot of **courage?** What types of courageous things
has he or she done?

5. How do you show your **appreciation** to other people?

6. What is something that you would *not* **be willing to** do, even for a good friend?
Why not?

WATCH

E ▶ **1.26** **WATCH FOR MAIN IDEAS** Watch the edited TED Talk by Kelly McGonigal. Then choose the correct to answer each question.

1. What is McGonigal's confession? What does she think she has done wrong?
   a. She has been teaching people that stress is good for them, but in fact it is not.
   b. She has put people's health in danger by telling them that stress is bad for their health.
   c. She has experienced a lot of stress.

2. What did McGonigal learn that changed her mind about stress?

   She learned that _____.
   a. stress has both harmful and beneficial effects on the body
   b. stress is very good for people
   c. the effects of stress on people's health depends on the way they think about stress

3. What are the possible benefits of stress?
   a. It can strengthen your heart and make you want to connect with other people.
   b. It can help you relax and live longer.
   c. It makes your heart beat faster and constricts the blood vessels.

4. What effect does taking care of people have on the brain? What is the connection between taking care of other people and stress?
   a. It causes the brain to release oxytocin, which helps protect us against the harmful effects of stress.
   b. It has a similar effect on the brain as other major stressful life experiences.
   c. Taking care of people is stressful, so the brain becomes more resilient.

5. What is the main purpose of McGonigal's talk?
   a. She wants to change the way people think about stress so that they can benefit from it, rather than be harmed by it.
   b. She wants to convince people to take better care of themselves so that they do not suffer from as many stress-related health problems.
   c. She wants people to be thankful for the stressful experiences in their lives and share them with other people.

NOTE-TAKING SKILL Use Symbols

To show the relationships between ideas, use symbols when you take notes. It will allow you to take notes more quickly.

Causes and Effect	Similarity and Difference		Amount/Increase and Decrease	
Cause X $\longrightarrow$ Y	the same	=	increase/go up	$\uparrow$
Effect Y $\longleftarrow$ X	more than	>	decrease/go down	$\downarrow$
	less than	<		

F ▶ **1.27** **WATCH FOR DETAILS** Watch the segments from the edited TED Talk and fill in the blanks in the notes with symbols from the Note-Taking Skill box. In some cases, more than one symbol might be correct.

Segment 1: Study 1

30,000 U.S. adults for 8 yrs.

Qs: How much stress in last year? AND Do you believe stress is harmful?

RESULTS = People experience a lot of stress & believe stress is harmful

43% _____↑_____ risk of dying
     1

BUT only true if people believe stress is harmful. People NOT believe

stress is harmful, had no _____↓_____ risk of dying—they had lowest risk of dying!
                          2

Believing stress is bad for you _____=_____ 15th largest cause of death, _____>_____
                                3   4

skin cancer, HIV/AIDS, & homicide

Segment 2: Built-In Mechanism for Stress Resilience = Human Connection

reach out to others under stress _____>_____ ↑ release oxytocin _____>_____
                                 5   6

healthier stress response _____>_____ recover faster from stress
                          7

G **TALK ABOUT CAUSE AND EFFECT** Work with a partner. Each student will explain the notes from one of the segments in exercise F. Speak in full sentences. Use signal words and phrases from the Speaking Skill and Listening Skill boxes in Part 1 where possible.

H ▶ **1.28** **EXPAND YOUR VOCABULARY** Watch the excerpts from the TED Talk. Guess the meanings of the phrases in the box.

> freak (someone) out   fine-tune   bottle (something) up
> change one's mind   nudge   reach out to

I **WATCH MORE** Go to TED.com to watch the full TED Talk by Kelly McGonigal.

AFTER YOU WATCH

J COMMUNICATE Work in a small group. Read Kelly McGonigal's idea worth spreading. Then discuss the questions below.

> Kelly McGonigal's idea worth spreading is if we can view stress as our body's natural (and even positive!) reaction to a difficult situation, it's far better for our relationships, health, and happiness.

1. What was most surprising to you about the information in McGonigal's talk? Why was it surprising?

2. Has a social interaction ever helped you deal with a stressful situation? If yes, explain what happened.

K THINK CRITICALLY Analyze. Work in a small group. Read the following quotes from famous people. Discuss how they relate to Kelly McGonigal's talk and her idea worth spreading. Then share your ideas with the class.

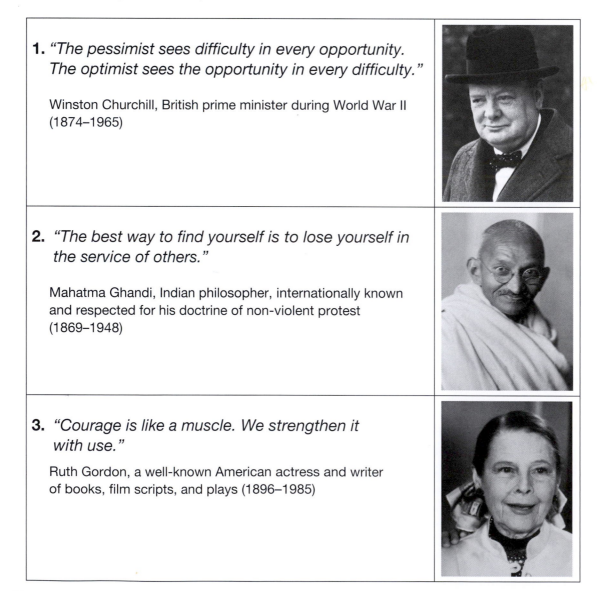

1. *"The pessimist sees difficulty in every opportunity. The optimist sees the opportunity in every difficulty."*

   Winston Churchill, British prime minister during World War II (1874–1965)

2. *"The best way to find yourself is to lose yourself in the service of others."*

   Mahatma Ghandi, Indian philosopher, internationally known and respected for his doctrine of non-violent protest (1869–1948)

3. *"Courage is like a muscle. We strengthen it with use."*

   Ruth Gordon, a well-known American actress and writer of books, film scripts, and plays (1896–1985)

Put It Together

A THINK CRITICALLY **Synthesize.** Work in a small group. Check [✓] all of the statements that you believe are true about the lecture in Part 1 and/or the edited TED Talk in Part 2. As you discuss the information, refer back to specific information from the lecture and the talk to support your answers.

1. _____ The talks have very similar main ideas.

2. _____ Some of the information in the lecture is repeated in the talk.

3. _____ They deal with the same topic but discuss different aspects of it.

4. _____ The speakers probably have different attitudes toward stress.

5. _____ The lecturer probably has not read the studies that McGonigal refers to.

6. _____ McGonigal does not know as much about stress as the lecturer does.

COMMUNICATE

ASSIGNMENT: Conduct a Survey. You are going to conduct a survey on stress and prepare a group presentation to report the results of the survey. Review the ideas in Parts 1 and 2 and the listening and speaking skills as you prepare for your presentation.

PREPARE

PRESENTATION SKILL **Vary Your Pace**

Varying the pace of your speech in a presentation can help you emphasize an important, interesting, or unexpected piece of information. It can also help you create drama and suspense so that your audience is eagerly waiting for what you will say next. You can vary your pace by . . .

- using pauses before and after the information you want to emphasize. These pauses should be longer than the pauses you normally use.

- slowing down your pace just before you get to the information you want to emphasize and then speaking slowly when you give that information.

▶ **1.29** Watch and read the excerpt from the TED Talk. Notice how the speaker varies her pace.

I want to tell you about one of the most under-appreciated aspects of the stress response, and the idea is this: Stress makes you social.

To understand this side of stress, we need to talk about a hormone, oxytocin.

Passengers on a ferry, Georgia
Strait, British Columbia, Canada

B ▶ **1.30** Watch the excerpt from the TED Talk two times. The first time, underline
the places where the speaker starts to slow down. The second time, mark
each pause you hear with a slash [/] and double underline the most important
information.

> *And when you choose to view stress in this way, you're not just getting better at*
> *stress, you're actually making a pretty profound statement. You're saying that you*
> *can trust yourself to handle life's challenges. And you're remembering that you*
> *don't have to face them alone.*

C Compare your markings with those of your classmates. If your markings are
different, watch again.

D Work in a group. Prepare for your presentation. Follow these steps.

1. Look at the survey on page 101. Each person in your group should have at least
   five people (not from your class) take the survey. You should ask the questions
   orally and record the responses you get directly on the survey by writing an *X* for
   each response. Then count the responses for each question.

2. Decide what the results might mean. What conclusions, if any, can you make?
   Think about whether the results support what McGonigal says in her talk.

3. Organize your presentation. In it, you should:

   • Report what the results were (e.g., *6 out of 8 people answered* True *to*
     question 1).

   • Then make logical conclusions based on the results.

   • Discuss how the results support (or don't support) what McGonigal says
     in her talk.

4. Assign a part of the presentation to each member of the group.

Stress Survey

I am conducting a survey on stress for a class presentation. I would appreciate it if you could help me by answering the following questions. Thank you very much!

Are these statements true or false? Answer *true* or *false* for each statement. If you are not sure, give your best guess.

1. Stress is almost always bad for your health.   True _____✓_____   False _____
2. Stress can save your life.   True _____~_____   False _____
3. Stress can kill you.   True _____✓_____   False _____
4. Stress can help you make contact with other people.   True _____✓_____   False _____
5. Your attitude toward stress is more important than your actual level of stress.   True _____✓_____   False _____

E Read the rubric on page 181. Notice how your presentation will be evaluated. Keep these categories in mind as you present and as you watch your classmates' presentations.

PRESENT

F Give your presentation to the class. After your group presents, listen to the other groups' presentations and evaluate them.

G **THINK CRITICALLY** **Evaluate.** In your group, discuss the feedback you received. As a class, discuss what each group did well and what might make each presentation even stronger.

REFLECT

Reflect on what you have learned. Check [✓] your progress.

I can
- [ ] listen for and recognize cause and effect.
- [ ] talk about causes and effects using appropriate signal words and phrases.
- [ ] recognize and speak in thought groups.
- [ ] use symbols when note taking.
- [ ] vary my pace in order to emphasize certain information or ideas.

speaking presentation

I understand the meanings of these words and phrases and can use them.
Circle those you know. Underline those you need to work on.

access AWL	confession	heal	release AWL
appreciation AWL	courage	inevitably AWL	reveal AWL
be associated with	crisis	mechanism AWL	resilience
chronic	empathy	motivate AWL	strengthen
compassionate	enhance AWL	muscle	be willing to (do something)

UNIT 6
Treasured Places

Tourists visit King Tut's funerary mask in
Cairo's Egyptian Museum, Cairo, Egypt.

THINK AND DISCUSS

1 Look at the photo. Describe what you see. Would you like to visit this place? Why, or why not?

2 Read the unit title. What does the word *treasured* mean? How do you think the title and the photo are related? What do you think the unit is going to be about?

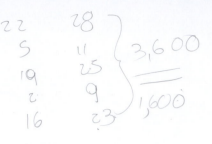

PART 1 A Precious Resource

BEFORE YOU LISTEN

A COMMUNICATE Work in a small group. Discuss these questions.

1. Look at the photo and read the Part 1 title. What does the word *precious* mean? What do you think the "precious resource" referred to in the title is?

2. Have you ever gone scuba diving or snorkeling? If so, tell your group about your experience. If not, would you like to? Why, or why not?

B THINK CRITICALLY Predict. Work in a small group. Discuss the questions and predict the answers that you will hear in the class discussion. Use a dictionary to look up any unfamiliar words.

1. What are coral reefs, and why are they important to the health of the ocean?

2. What is happening to coral reefs today?

3. How do coral reefs benefit humans?

Great Barrier Reef, Australia

VOCABULARY

C 🎧 **2.9** Read and listen to the sentences with words from the class discussion. Guess the meaning of each bold word. Then write each word next to its definition.

a. There was a **massive** oil spill in the Gulf of Mexico. It was one of the largest environmental disasters in history.

b. Some kinds of shellfish are able to **cement** themselves to hard objects, such as rocks and the bottoms of boats. It's very difficult to remove them.

c. That movie was **instrumental** in getting the public to pay attention to the issue of global warming. Before then, nobody seemed to know or care about the issue.

d. Some animals can survive in a variety of **habitats,** but others can live in only one very specific kind of place.

e. There are many different **species** of fish, of all different colors, shapes, and sizes.

f. Coral can survive a certain amount of pollution, but they won't **thrive.** They will be unhealthy and will eventually start to die.

g. The **preservation** of our planet is everyone's responsibility. If we do not work together, we will destroy the environment and our children's future.

h. I believe that life is **precious.** That is why I teach my children to respect all living things.

i. The coral is extremely **fragile.** When you are swimming, be careful not to touch it with your hands or feet. Just a slight touch can damage or even kill it.

j. Before they put up the **barrier,** the river used to flood the road every time it rained. Now it only floods when it rains unusually hard for several days.

1. _cement_ (v) attach firmly

2. _barrier_ (n) something that blocks the way

3. _habitats_ (n) the areas in which animals and plants normally live

4. _instrumental_ (adj) helpful; causing something to happen

5. _species_ (n) groupings of living things

6. _fragile_ (adj) easily broken or harmed

7. _thrive_ (v) grow strong and healthy

8. _precious_ (adj) extremely valuable and well loved

9. _massive_ (adj) huge; great in number or size

10. _preservation_ (n) protection from harm or change

An orangutan hugs a kitten. Sometimes animals of different species form "friendships."

D **COMMUNICATE** Work with a partner. Answer the questions. Use the words in bold in your answers.

1. Which interests you most: different **species** of fish, birds, insects, or mammals? Why?

2. What can humans do to preserve the natural **habitats** of animal species that are in danger of extinction, for example, orangutans and panda bears?

3. Who has played an **instrumental** role in your education? Explain how.

4. Is the **preservation** of cultural traditions more difficult today than in the past? Why, or why not?

LISTEN

E 🎧 **2.10** **LISTEN FOR MAIN IDEAS** Listen to the class discussion. Check [✓] the main idea.

1. _____ People should take responsibility for their role in damaging coral reefs.

2. _____ The preservation of coral reefs is important for both marine and human life.

3. _____ Many species of marine life will die if steps are not taken to preserve coral reefs.

4. _____ The economic impact of damage to coral reefs is massive.

WORDS IN THE CLASS DISCUSSION
Bingo: slang for "That's exactly right."
critter (n): an informal, affectionate word for a living creature such as an insect

F 🎧 **2.11** **LISTEN FOR DETAILS** Read the list of topics and supporting information. Then listen to an excerpt from the class discussion and write the letter of each piece of supporting information next to the correct topic.

Topics

1. What a coral reef is and how it is formed _____

2. How coral reefs contribute to the ocean's health _____

3. Coral reefs in danger _____

Supporting Information

    a. 20 percent of reefs dying

    b. overfishing

    c. attract fish and shellfish

    d. pollution

    e. polyps attach to hard surface

    f. 50 percent of reefs at risk

    g. produce chemical and stick together to form reef

    h. provide 25 percent of marine species with food and habitat

    i. global warming

An anemonefish inside its host sea anemone on Three Sisters Reef, Australia

---

NOTE-TAKING SKILL Rewrite Your Notes in Outline Form

It is important to not only take notes in class but also organize and rewrite your notes after the lecture. Otherwise, you probably won't be able to understand your notes when you need to study them for a test or exam.

🎧 **2.12** Listen to an excerpt from the class discussion and look at the notes.

Coral—diff types

Reefs = hard coral—hard, but NOT rocks, animals
1 piece = coral polyp float, attach hrd surface = home (if good loc)

Polyps release chem, (calcium carb) ⟶ hard skel?? (like bone)
+ cements polyps togthr ⟶ coral reef, oldst 50M yrs, lgst Grt. Barrier Reef in Aus, 230km

Now look at the same notes, rewritten and reorganized into a simple outline.

I. How coral reefs are formed:

    A. hard coral (animal) 1 piece = coral polyp

    B. polyps attach to hard surface & release calcium carbonate

    C. calc carb cemnts polyps together & makes coral reef

    D. oldst coral reef = 50M yrs.

    E. lgst reef = Grt Barrier Reef in Aus, 230 km long

G  **2.13 LISTEN AND TAKE NOTES** Listen to the segment from the discussion and complete the notes.

Topic = Importance of _____
                                   1

_____ industry: _____ people depend on reefs for
           2   3

_____ or _____
           4   5

_____ shoreline—: _____ btw ocean & _____,
           6   7   8

_____ damage to land
           9

_____ —: snorkeling & _____
          10   11

_____ research: _____ cancer, HIV drugs (developed from
          12   13

plants + animals on reefs)

_____ to world economy: $ _____ / year
          14   15

H **REWRITE YOUR NOTES** Complete the outline with information from your notes in exercise G. Then work with a partner and compare your outlines.

Topic = The Importance of _____*coral reefs to human life*_____

A. _____

B. _____

C. _____

D. _____

E. _____

Divers collecting coral samples
from Great Barrier Reef, Australia

LISTENING SKILL Recognize Linking

Within a thought group, speakers often link the end of one word to the beginning of the next word. However, we do not usually link the end of one thought group to the next. Read and listen to the example.

🎧 **2.14**

Let me put it another way. What happens if you take away a species' habitat?

They can't **thrive.** In fact, many of them won't even survive.

Linking can make it hard to distinguish all of the words in a thought group. Some of the unstressed words almost disappear. This makes the stressed word stand out more and can make two or more words sound like one word. If you are aware of linking, you can train your ear to listen for it. With time and practice, you will be able to hear each word.

I 🎧 **2.15** Listen to an excerpt from the class discussion. Fill in the blanks with the missing words. You will hear the excerpt twice.

TA: What makes _____ _____ instrumental _____
                               1   2   3

_____ _____ ?
     4   5

Student: They provide _____ for _____ _____
                              6   7   8

_____ .
     9

TA: Good, but _____ _____ _____ that idea
                          10   11   12

_____ _____ _____ _____ ?
     13   14   15   16

J 🎧 **2.16** Listen and write the sentences you hear. You will hear each sentence three times.

1. _____

2. _____

3. _____

AFTER YOU LISTEN

K **THINK CRITICALLY Analyze.** Work in a small group. Compare your sentences from exercises I and J. Which words did you miss? Did you miss more stressed or unstressed words?

L THINK CRITICALLY **Interpret an Infographic.** Work in a group. Look at the infographic and answer the questions that follow.

10 Tips for Protecting Coral Reefs

1 Corals are already a **GIFT**. Don't give them as presents.

2 **EDUCATE** yourself about coral reefs and the sea life they support.

3 Use **ENERGY EFFICIENT LIGHT BULBS**. They reduce greenhouse gas emissions. Climate change is one of the leading threats to coral reef survival.

4 Choose **SUSTAINABLE SEAFOOD**.

5 If you scuba dive, **DON'T TOUCH**.

6 When you learn about coral reefs, you can **TEACH OTHERS** about the importance of the world's coral reefs.

7 **DON'T PUT CHEMICALS** into our oceans. Certain chemicals and nutrients increase the growth of algae that prevent sunlight from reaching coral.

8 **SAVE WATER.** The less water you use, the less polluted water goes back into the ocean.

9 **VOLUNTEER!** Help clean up your local beach or coral reef.

10 Practice **SAFE BOATING.** Stay away from coral reefs and areas with sea grass.

Source: NOAA

1. Who is the audience for this infographic? In other words, who was the infographic written for?

2. According to the class discussion, what are the three reasons why coral reefs are at risk? Write them in the left column of the chart. A fourth risk not mentioned in the discussion is included in the left column.

PROBLEMS	TIPS ON HOW YOU CAN HELP
1.	
2.	
3.	
4. ocean recreation	

3. Look at the infographic. Which of the problems from the chart in question 2 are the tips in the infographic meant to address? Write the number of each tip from the infographic in the right column, next to the appropriate problem. For some problems, there may be more than one tip.

4. Which of the things in the infographic do you already do? Which (if any) might you do now that you understand the importance of coral reefs?

A fisherman throwing his anchor into a lagoon,
Aitutaki Island, Cook Islands

M COMMUNICATE Work in a group. You have just learned about an environmental problem that could affect our future. What are some other problems in the world today that could affect our future? Which of these problems, if any, are you most interested in helping solve? Why? Share your answers with your group.

SPEAKING

SPEAKING SKILL	Ask For and Give Clarification

Learning polite language to ask for and give clarification is very important. Here are some polite expressions for asking for and giving clarification and for checking understanding.

Asking For Clarification	Checking Your Understanding	Making Sure That Others Understand You
Sorry, I didn't catch that. Could you repeat it? I'm not sure I understand the question. Sorry, I'm not following you.	Are you saying that . . . Do you mean that . . . If I understand correctly, you're saying that . . . , right? Oh, now I get it. You're talking about . . . , right?	Are you following me? Are you with me? Have you got it? Do you see how . . . ? Let me clarify. Let me put it another way.

See page 167 of the *Independent Student Handbook* for more expressions used to ask for, check, and give clarification.

There are several different types of questions. Read and listen to the examples from the class discussion. Notice the intonation pattern for each type of question.

🎧 **2.17**

***Wh-* (Information) Questions:**

What happens if you take away a species' **hab**itat?

One-Word Questions:

How?

***Yes/No* Questions:**

Has everyone **got** it?

Statement Questions:

They protect the **shore**line?

N 🎧 **2.18** Listen and check [✓] the type of question you hear. Then listen again and repeat the question after the speaker.

1. _____ *yes/no* question   _____ information question   _____ statement question

2. _____ *yes/no* question   _____ information question   _____ statement question

3. _____ *yes/no* question   _____ information question   _____ statement question

O **COMMUNICATE** Work with a partner. Take turns asking and answering the questions below. You can look back at pages 107–108 to help you remember the information. Use clarifying language and appropriate question intonation.

1. Are corals plants? How is a coral reef formed?

2. How do coral reefs contribute to the health of the oceans?

3. What is happening to coral reefs today?

4. Why are coral reefs so important to the world economy?

P **THINK CRITICALLY** **Apply.** Work in a small group. Imagine that the people listed in the box below live in a seaside community with a coral reef close to the shore. The reef is currently healthy, and everyone wants it to stay that way. Discuss what each person can do to ensure the preservation of the reef. Use questions and clarifying language as necessary.

an artist	a scuba diver	a marine biologist	an elementary school teacher
the director of a local museum		a local fisherman	the owner of a local tour company

An underwater art museum, teeming with life

" Our oceans are sacred. "

BEFORE YOU WATCH

A   Read the title and the information about the TED speaker. What do you think "teeming with life" means? Why does the speaker call the oceans "sacred"? Discuss your ideas with a partner.

JASON DECAIRES TAYLOR   Sculptor

For sculptor Jason deCaires Taylor, the ocean is more than inspiration for his art. It is an exhibition space and museum. Taylor creates sculptures and sinks them to the ocean floor. There they are transformed from lifeless stone into habitats for an amazing variety of ocean life.

Underwater sculptures by
Jason deCaires Taylor
off the coast of Cancún, Mexico

B **COMMUNICATE** Work with a partner. Discuss these questions.

1. Where does the TED speaker exhibit his art? Who do you think sees it?

2. If you put a sculpture made of stone on the floor of the ocean, how would it change? Describe what you think might happen to it.

C The TED speaker mentions the following famous places in his talk. Work with a partner. Complete the sentences with the letter of the correct answer.

1. La Sagrada Familia is a church designed by the architect Gaudí in _____.
   a. Italy   **b.** Spain   **c.** Portugal

2. The Himalayas are a range of mountains that include _____.
   a. Mt. Fuji   **b.** The Andes   **c.** Mt. Everest

3. The Sistine Chapel is a church whose ceiling was painted by _____.
   a. Leonardo da Vinci   **b.** Michelangelo   **c.** Pablo Picasso

D **THINK CRITICALLY** **Predict.** Work with a partner. Check the images that you think you will see in the edited TED Talk.

1. _____ a coral reef

2. _____ a museum with photographs of sea plants and animals

3. _____ fish and shellfish living inside a sculpture

4. _____ Jason deCaires Taylor making a sculpture on the ocean floor

5. _____ scuba divers looking at underwater sculptures

6. _____ trash floating on the surface of the ocean

VOCABULARY

E 🎧 **2.19** The sentences and quotes below will help you learn words and phrases in the edited TED Talk. Read and listen to the sentences and guess the meanings of the words and phrases in bold. Then write T for *true* and F for false for the statements that follow. Correct the false statements to make them true.

1. "As soon as we **submerge** the sculptures, they're not ours anymore because as soon as we sink them, the sculptures, they belong to the sea."

   _F_ When you **submerge** something, you put part of it underwater.

2. Jason deCaires Taylor uses materials and designs that create a **stable** environment for sea plants and animals to grow on and thrive.

   _F_ A **stable** environment is uncertain and always changing.

3. Jason deCaires Taylor creates **textured** surfaces on his sculptures so that sea life can easily attach to them.

   _F_ A **textured** surface is smooth, not rough.

4. The ocean **currents** move coral polyps from the natural reefs to the underwater sculptures, where they can attach themselves and live.

   _T_ **Currents** are flows of something, such as water or electricity.

5. "Since building these sites, we've seen some **phenomenal** and unexpected results."

   _T_ **Phenomenal** results are extraordinary.

6. "The sculpture park in Grenada was instrumental in the government **designating** a spot a marine-protected area."

   _F_ Governments **designate** certain areas as protected in order to preserve the environment there.

7. "When we see these incredible places and things . . . we do our best to **cherish** them, to protect them and to keep them safe."

   _____ People who **cherish** nature are less likely to protect the environment than people who don't.

8. "[The ocean is] simply too massive, too **vast**, too endless. . . . I think most people actually look past to the **horizon**."

   _F_ **Vast** means small and unimportant.

   _T_ The **horizon** is the line where the ocean appears to meet the sky.

9. "I hope that by bringing our art into the ocean, . . . we are also giving something back, and by encouraging new environments to thrive, and . . . opening up a new . . . way of seeing the seas: as . . . precious places, **worthy of** our protection."

   _____ Something that is **worthy of** protection is valuable and therefore should be protected.

F COMMUNICATE Use the scale to indicate how strongly you agree or disagree with each of the statements below. Then with a partner, take turns explaining your answers. Use the words in bold in your answers.

1 = strongly disagree   2 = disagree   3 = agree   4 = strongly agree

1. _____ My most recent vacation was **phenomenal**.

2. _____ I think that governments should **designate** more natural areas as protected.

3. _____ If we do not teach our children to **cherish** nature, we will never be able to solve our environmental problems.

4. _____ The harm to coral reefs is **worthy of** more media attention.

5. _____ **Submerging** sculptures in the ocean is a great idea.

WATCH

G ▶ **1.31** **WATCH FOR MAIN IDEAS** Read the question and possible answers about the edited TED Talk by Jason deCaires Taylor. Then watch the talk and check the three statements that answer the question.

Why does deCaires Taylor call the sites where he places his sculptures "museums"?

1. __T__ People respect museums and value the things that are in them.

2. __T__ He wants people to respect the oceans as much as they respect museums so that they will protect them from environmental damage.

3. __T__ Museums have a lot of ancient objects that teach people about the past.

4. __T__ Museums are a well-respected educational resource.

5. __F__ He thinks his sculptures are good enough to be exhibited in a museum.

WORDS IN THE TALK
configured (v): arranged in a special way
decimated (v): completely destroyed
spawn (v): lay eggs
veins (n): blood vessels that bring blood to the heart and lungs

An above-surface view of a coral reef, Isla Mujeres, Mexico

H ▶ **1.32** **WATCH FOR DETAILS** Watch the segments from the edited TED Talk and choose the correct answer to each question.

Segment 1

1. When did the speaker put his first sculpture in the ocean?
   a. 10 years ago   **b.** 2 years ago   **c.** 20 years ago

2. Where was the speaker's first underwater sculpture park?
   a. a dive center   **b.** Grenada   **c.** Hurricane Ivan

Segment 2

3. How many sculptures are there in the underwater museum in Mexico?
   a. 16   **b.** 40   **c.** more than 500

4. Where is the first underwater botanical garden in the Atlantic Ocean going to be?
   a. the Bahamas   **b.** Lanzarote   **c.** Ocean Atlas

Segment 3

5. How do the speaker's sculptures help sea life to thrive?
   a. by protecting them from large, dangerous fish
   b. by providing them with a place to live
   c. by keeping them away from coral reefs

Segment 4

6. Why does the speaker mention the Himalayas, La Sagrada Familia, The Sistine Chapel, and the Grand Canyon?
   a. He is comparing the oceans to places we value and protect.
   b. He wants to explain why we pollute the oceans.
   c. They are in famous museums around the world.

I ▶ **1.33** **EXPAND YOUR VOCABULARY** Watch the excerpts from the TED Talk. Guess the meanings of the phrases in the box.

steep learning curve	take up	plug into
team up with	blow one's mind	wreak havoc

J **WATCH MORE** Go to TED.com to watch the full TED Talk by Jason deCaires Taylor.

AFTER YOU WATCH

The Banker by Jason deCaires Taylor

K **THINK CRITICALLY** **Analyze and Reflect.** Work in a group. Read Jason deCaires Taylor's idea worth spreading. Based on your understanding of his idea and edited TED Talk, the image above, and your own opinions, discuss the questions below with your group.

> Jason deCaires Taylor's idea worth spreading is that by bringing our art into the ocean we can take advantage of the stunning visual impact of the setting and also help restore marine habitats and encourage people to see the oceans as precious places worthy of protection.

1. What or who does the sculpture in the image from deCaires Taylor's talk represent? How does it relate to his idea worth spreading? Why do you think it is the most commonly shared image of deCaires Taylor's work?

2. Do you agree with deCaires Taylor's idea worth spreading? Do you think it will encourage people to get involved in protecting the oceans? Explain your answers.

3. In your opinion, which five of the words in the box below best describe deCaires Taylor's sculptures? Choose only five. Then add your own idea and get together with another group and compare and explain your choices.

> absurd   beautiful   educational   fragile   innovative
> phenomenal   precious   scary   strange   unique
>
> Your idea: _____

4. Do you like deCaires Taylor's art? What do you like or dislike about it? Would you like to see it in person? Why, or why not?

Put It Together

A THINK CRITICALLY Synthesize. Work in a small group. You will participate in a class competition. Follow these steps:

1. As a group, think of as many similarities and differences as you can between the teaching assistant in Part 1 and the TED speaker in Part 2. Consider their work, their beliefs, their personalities, their interests, and anything else you can think of. You will have 15 minutes. Your teacher will tell you when to stop.

2. Share your group's lists of similarities and differences with the class. If another group challenges any of your answers, you must be ready to defend the comparison.

3. Determine which group came up with the most similarities and differences.

COMMUNICATE

ASSIGNMENT: Participate in a Group Discussion You will participate in a group discussion. Then you will observe your classmates' group discussion and evaluate their performance. Review the ideas in Parts 1 and 2 and the listening and speaking skills as you prepare for your discussion.

PREPARE

PRESENTATION SKILL **Be an Active Participant in a Discussion**

Participating in a group discussion is easy for some students and difficult for others. Here are some guidelines that will help the discussion go smoothly for everyone.

- Listen carefully to what others say, and make sure they are finished before you begin speaking. Don't interrupt.*
- Ask for clarification if you are not sure about something.
- Look at other participants when you speak. If they look confused, check their understanding.
- Build on other participants' contributions by briefly referring to their ideas and then adding your own. For example, "*I agree with what Ali said about _____. In addition, I think that . . .*"
- Make sure everyone in the group has the chance to express their ideas.
- If someone is not participating, ask him or her a question. For example, "*Anthony, what do you think about what Maria just said?*"

(*See page 167 of the *Independent Student Handbook* for more information about interrupting politely.)

University students collect trash
at Bagan Lalang Beach, Malaysia.

B Prepare for your group discussion. Your teacher will assign you to Group A or B.
Group A will discuss topic A while Group B listens and evaluates. Then Group B will
discuss topic B while Group A listens and evaluates.

> **Group A's Discussion Topic:** What can individuals do to protect the environment?
> Be specific. How effective are these actions? Explain your answers with examples.

> **Group B's Discussion Topic:** What are various governments doing to protect the
> environment? Be specific. Which actions are most effective, in your opinion? Least
> effective? What more could they be doing?

Follow these steps as you prepare for your discussion.

1. Read and think about your discussion topic. Write notes on what you would like
   to say during the discussion.

2. Your teacher will assign one of the following roles to each person in your group.
   Do not show your role to anyone else.

> **Role 1:** Get the discussion started by asking a question. Keep the discussion
> going if it starts to slow down or stops.

> **Role 2:** Make sure everyone is participating. Ask questions of students who are
> not talking to get them involved in the discussion.

> **Role 3:** Make sure that everyone is following the discussion. Check in occasionally
> by asking if people are following. Watch your classmates' faces; if anyone looks
> confused, clarify or ask the speaker to clarify.

PRESENT

C Follow these steps:

1. Read the rubric on page 181. Notice how your group's discussion will be evaluated. Keep these categories in mind as you participate in your group discussion.

2. Students in Group A sit in a circle and participate in the discussion. Make sure you understand and perform your role from step 2. Also, remember the guidelines in the Presentation Skill box.

3. Students in Group B sit in the outside circle and observe the discussion. Listen carefully and try to guess which role each student in Group A has. Do not speak, but you can take notes if you like.

4. After 10–15 minutes, your teacher will stop the discussion and ask the students in Group B to say which role each student in Group A had and evaluate the discussion using the rubric on page 181.

5. Groups now change positions. Repeat steps 2–4 above.

D After you observe, provide feedback to the group that participated in the discussion. Use the rubric as a guide. Add notes or any other feedback you want to share.

E **THINK CRITICALLY Evaluate.** In your group, discuss the feedback you received. Discuss what your group did well and what could have made your group discussion even stronger.

REFLECT

Reflect on what you have learned. Check [✓] your progress.

I can
- ☐ rewrite my notes in outline form.
- ☐ recognize linking.
- ☐ ask for and give clarification and check understanding.
- ☐ recognize and use correct question intonation.
- ☐ participate actively in a group discussion.

I understand the meanings of these words and can use them.
Circle those you know. Underline those you need to work on.

barrier	fragile	phenomenal AWL	submerge
cement	habitat	precious	textured
cherish	horizon	preservation	thrive
current	instrumental	species	vast
designate	massive	stable AWL	worthy of

National Geographic Explorer, pilot, and educator Barrington Irving with his Experience Aviation students on the plane Barrington flew on his 2007 record-breaking flight around the world. He was 23 years old at the time, making him the youngest person (and the first African American) to fly solo around the globe.

UNIT **7**

Live and Learn

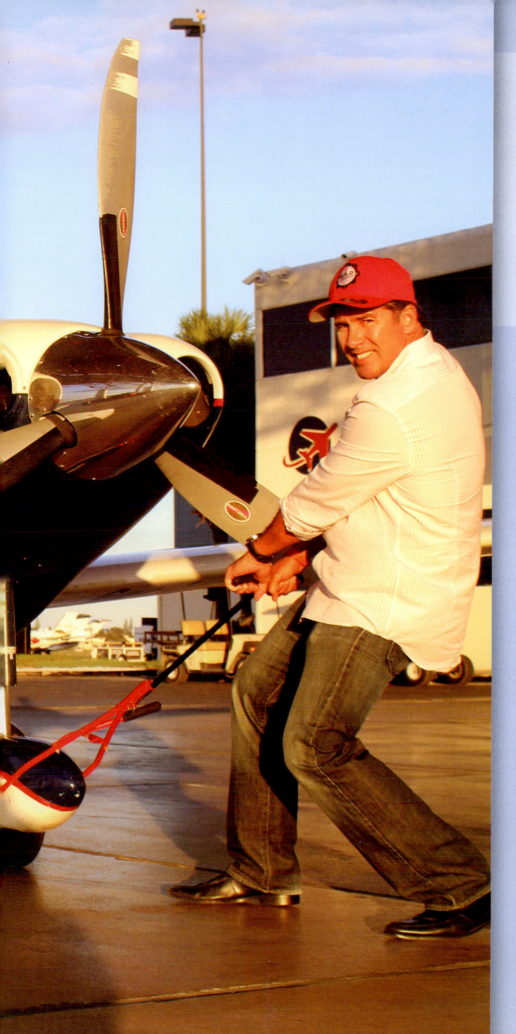

THINK AND DISCUSS

1 Look at the photo and read the caption. What do you think the students in this photo are learning about? Would you like to be one of Barrington Irving's students? Why, or why not?

2 Read the unit title. What do you think the unit is going to be about?

PART 1   Is the Internet Making Us Bad Readers?

BEFORE YOU LISTEN

A   COMMUNICATE Work in a small group. Discuss these questions.

1. Read the title. How would you answer the question in the title? Why?

2. Read the definition of a roundtable discussion. Then answer the questions that follow.

> A *roundtable discussion* is a discussion among several experts, often on a topic of interest to the community. The experts are chosen to represent a range of points of view on the topic. It is called a "roundtable" discussion because the participants sit at a round table and exchange ideas about the topic. Often, the discussion is broadcast on television or radio, and members of the community can call in and share their points of view.

Have you ever watched, listened to, or participated in a roundtable discussion? If so, what was the topic and why were you asked to participate? If not, are such discussions common in your country on television or radio? Do you like to watch or listen to them?

B   2.20 THINK CRITICALLY Predict. Work in a group. Read the Part 1 title again. What kinds of professionals and members of the community do you think will be involved in the roundtable discussion on this topic? Discuss your ideas. Then listen to the introduction to the roundtable discussion and check your predictions.

A boy uses an iPad while the other reads a book.

VOCABULARY

C 🎧 **2.21** Read and listen to the sentences with words and phrases from the roundtable discussion. Guess the meaning of each bold word or phrase. Then write each word or phrase next to its definition.

   a. Computers have **impacted** our lives in many ways. Life today is completely different than it was 50 years ago, and many of the changes are due to computers.

   b. My daughter is academically **gifted**. She was able to graduate from high school three years early and started university when she was only 15.

   c. The Internet has existed for a few **decades**, but most people didn't start to use it until about 25 years ago.

   d. If I need to concentrate on something for an **extended** period of time, I turn off all of my electronic devices and go somewhere quiet.

   e. At first I was not convinced that the Internet was a good thing, but **on balance** I've decided that it has done more good than harm.

   f. **There is no doubt** that both teaching and learning have been affected by the Internet.

   g. That is completely **absurd**! You don't know what you are talking about. How could a computer be more intelligent than a human being?

   h. Cell phones become **outdated** very quickly. I replace mine every two years.

   i. No matter how old they are, teachers should be **up-to-date** on the latest technology.

   j. My grandmother never lost her sense of **wonder** about the world. She was always curious and young at heart.

1. _____ (n) amazement and joy

2. _____ (adj) continued

3. _____ (adj) having a special natural ability

4. _____ (v) affected; influenced

5. _____ (n) periods of 10 years

6. _____ (adj) current; modern

7. _____ (adj) foolish; stupid

8. _____ (adj) no longer useful

9. _____ (phrase) It is certain; it is definitely true.

10. _____ (phrase) taking everything into consideration

D **COMMUNICATE** Work with a partner. Take turns asking and answering these questions. Use the words in bold in your answers.

1. What is something that you had a sense of **wonder** about as a child? Do you still have a sense of **wonder** about it? Why, or why not?

2. Other than your parents, who has **impacted** your life the most? Explain how he or she has **impacted** you.

3. In which country or city would you most like to spend an **extended** period of time? Explain why you chose that country or city. What would you like to do there?

4. When somebody expresses an opinion that you think is **absurd**, do you tend to say something, or do you remain silent? Why?

5. What are some things that become **outdated** within a few months? What are some things that take longer to become **outdated**?

6. What kinds of things do you like being **up-to-date** on? For example, do you like being **up-to-date** on the latest fashion trends? On technology? On current events? On movies? Explain why, or why not.

LISTEN

E 🎧 **2.22** **LISTEN FOR MAIN IDEAS** Read the statements. Then listen to the discussion. Check [✓] the six points of view that the speakers express.

1. _____ We need more research before we can say exactly how the Internet affects reading.

2. _____ The Internet sometimes makes people behave inappropriately.

3. _____ Young people are losing their ability to read because of the Internet.

4. _____ Young people do not understand why they should memorize information.

5. _____ Because the Internet has written text as well as pictures and videos, it makes reading easier for some students.

6. _____ Young people read differently today than in the past.

7. _____ There are fewer printed books because young people don't buy them.

8. _____ By not reading deeply, young people are missing a lot.

F 🎧 **2.22** Listen again and identify which speaker expressed each point of view in exercise E. Write the number of the statement(s) next to the correct name. Some speakers have more than one point of view, and some share the same point of view.

Speakers

James Hall (reporter) _____   Pedro Martinez (teacher) _____

Melanie White (parent) _____   Katie Wang (student) _____

NOTE-TAKING SKILL Use a T-Chart to Take Notes

If a lecture, presentation, discussion, etc., deals with two sides of a topic (for example, positives and negatives, pros and cons, a comparison, or problems and solutions), using a T-chart can be a helpful way to organize your notes.

🎧 **2.23** Listen to the example and look at the notes in the T-chart.

THE EFFECT OF THE INTERNET ON STUDENTS' READING	
POSITIVE	**NEGATIVE**
Access lots of info immed. People read a lot on Internet	Internet use = lower concentration ↓ deep reading = diffclt bec. can't concntrate for long

G 🎧 **2.24** **LISTEN FOR DETAILS** Listen to a segment of the discussion and take notes in the T-chart.

THE EFFECT OF THE INTERNET ON STUDENTS' READING	
POSITIVE	**NEGATIVE**

LISTENING SKILL   Recognize a Speaker's Tone

Tone is the way that speakers use their voices to express their feelings and attitudes. For example, when speakers are excited, they often speak faster and louder, and their pitch (the tone of their voice) rises.

Tone and meaning are very closely related, so recognizing the speaker's tone is as important as understanding the words that he or she is saying.

Common Attitudes and Feelings Expressed Through Tone

anger	doubt	humor
certainty	enthusiasm	passion
compassion	frustration	sadness

🎧 **2.25** Read and listen to the example from the discussion. Pay attention to the speaker's tone.

Speaker's feeling: **enthusiasm**

> *Welcome to today's roundtable! Our subject today is the effect of the Internet on students' reading habits and comprehension. Please join me in welcoming our guests.*

H 🎧 **2.26** Listen to the segments from the discussion. Choose the words that express the speakers' attitudes or feelings.

Segment 1	Segment 2	Segment 3	Segment 4
a. anger	**a.** certainty	**a.** doubt	**a.** frustration
b. enthusiasm	**b.** humor	**b.** anger	**b.** doubt
c. sadness	**c.** anger	**c.** sadness	**c.** sadness

I 🎧 **2.26** Listen to the segments from the discussion again. Discuss your answers for each segment as a class.

Shakespeare and Company Bookstore,
Latin Quarter, Paris, France

AFTER YOU LISTEN

J Take the quiz. Choose your answer to each question.

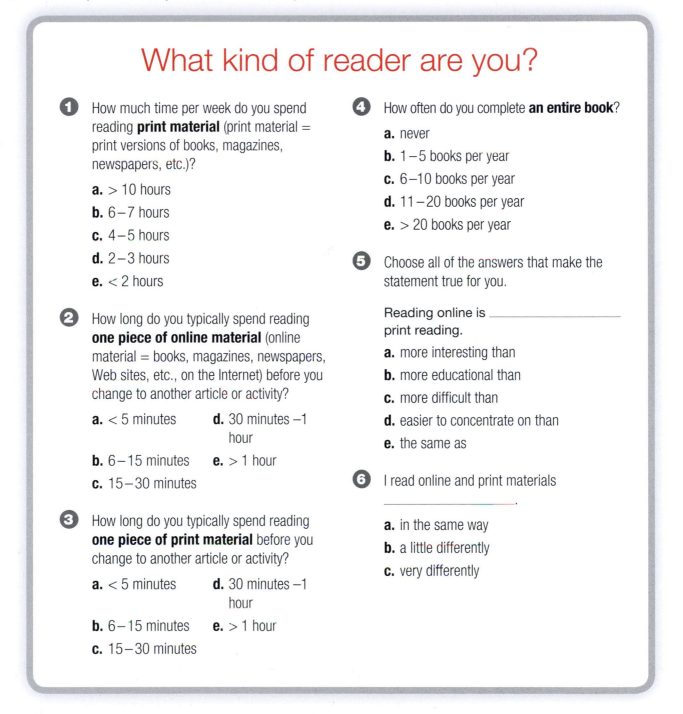

What kind of reader are you?

1 How much time per week do you spend reading **print material** (print material = print versions of books, magazines, newspapers, etc.)?

a. > 10 hours
b. 6–7 hours
c. 4–5 hours
d. 2–3 hours
e. < 2 hours

2 How long do you typically spend reading **one piece of online material** (online material = books, magazines, newspapers, Web sites, etc., on the Internet) before you change to another article or activity?

a. < 5 minutes   **d.** 30 minutes –1 hour
b. 6–15 minutes   **e.** > 1 hour
c. 15–30 minutes

3 How long do you typically spend reading **one piece of print material** before you change to another article or activity?

a. < 5 minutes   **d.** 30 minutes –1 hour
b. 6–15 minutes   **e.** > 1 hour
c. 15–30 minutes

4 How often do you complete **an entire book**?

a. never
b. 1–5 books per year
c. 6–10 books per year
d. 11–20 books per year
e. > 20 books per year

5 Choose all of the answers that make the statement true for you.

Reading online is _____ print reading.

a. more interesting than
b. more educational than
c. more difficult than
d. easier to concentrate on than
e. the same as

6 I read online and print materials _____

a. in the same way
b. a little differently
c. very differently

K **THINK CRITICALLY** **Evaluate.** Work in a group. Discuss these topics.

1. Compare and discuss your answers to the quiz. Explain your answers to questions 5 and 6.

2. Based on your answers to the quiz questions, your performance in school, and your own opinion, how would you rate your reading ability? Excellent? Good? Average? Below average? Explain your answer.

SPEAKING

SPEAKING SKILL Defend a Position

When you want to defend your position on a topic, you should clearly state your position using simple, declarative sentences (sentences that give facts or make statements). Then provide specific information that supports it. You can also use signal words and phrases to introduce and defend a position. Here are some examples:

One thing is clear . . .   It shouldn't be surprising that . . .   Research suggests . . .

There is no doubt that . . .   Many experts believe . . .   X seems to be (the key.)

🎧 **2.27** Read and listen to the example. Notice how the speaker uses a simple declarative sentence, a signal phrase, and specific information to support his position.

Everything we do affects the brain—exercise, food, whether we speak more than one language . . . the list is infinite. So it shouldn't be surprising or scary that the way we read affects the brain.

PRONUNCIATION SKILL Stress Key Words

Stress the key words in a sentence. Key words are usually content words (nouns, verbs, adjectives, adverbs, and the negative *no/not*) that communicate your main points.

To stress a key word, you should . . .

- make the vowel (*a, e, i, o, u*) in the stressed syllable of the key word longer than the vowels in other words in the same phrase.
- raise or lower the pitch (tone) on the key word.

🎧 **2.28** Read and listen to the example. Notice how the speaker clearly stresses the key words (in bold) when she states her position.

*And reading on the Internet is **fun**—I can read and watch videos related to what I'm **learning. Also**, because I'm a **visual** learner, the videos and pictures **help** me learn.*

L 🎧 **2.29** Read and listen to the excerpt from the discussion. Underline the signal words and phrases and double underline the key words. Then with a partner, take turns reading the excerpt. Make sure you stress the key words.

That said, research suggests that the Internet impacts our ability to concentrate on one thing over an extended period of time, say 30 minutes. This makes "deep reading"— —that is, concentrated reading, not just skimming quickly for information—more difficult.

A man reads near a fountain, Tokyo, Japan.

M **COMMUNICATE** Work with a partner. Follow these steps.

1. Read the statements in the box at the bottom of this page and choose a position to defend.

2. Prepare your argument.

3. Select one or two signal phrases from the Speaking Skill box to use in your argument.

4. Take turns stating and defending your position.

5. While you are presenting your argument, try to do the following:

   • Use simple, declarative sentences.
   • Support your position with specific information.
   • Use signal words and phrases.
   • Stress key words.

Statements

1. Reading books teaches you more than using the Internet.

2. Learning is easier today than it was in the past because of the Internet.

3. Classes where I can use a computer are more interesting than classes without computers.

4. Computers are not necessary in the classroom.

N THINK CRITICALLY Interpret an Infographic. Work in a group. Read the questions aloud. Then skim the infographic below to find the answers. Work as quickly as you can. Try to be the first group to finish. Your teacher will tell you when to begin.

1. What percent of people are good at multitasking?

2. According to the infographic, how much time will you save by not multitasking while studying?

3. What part of the brain do studying and social media use? How might this impact learning?

4. How can using social media while studying affect your grades?

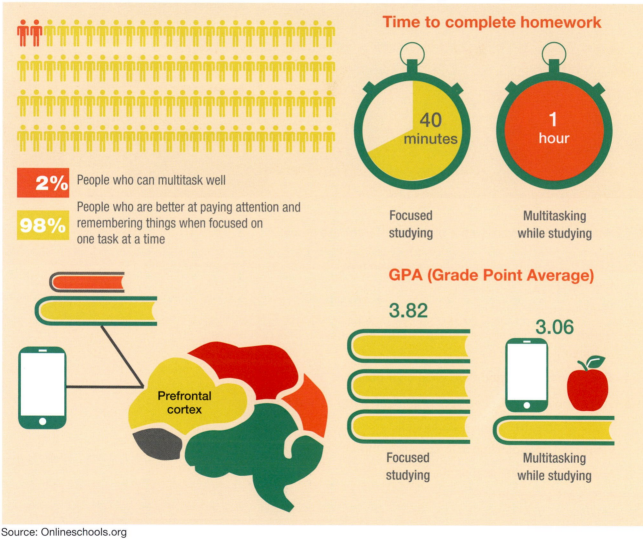

Do learning and multitasking go together?

2% People who can multitask well

98% People who are better at paying attention and remembering things when focused on one task at a time

Prefrontal cortex

Time to complete homework

40 minutes

1 hour

Focused studying

Multitasking while studying

GPA (Grade Point Average)

3.82

3.06

Focused studying

Multitasking while studying

Source: Onlineschools.org

A woman multitasks while having breakfast with her daughter.

O **THINK CRITICALLY** **Personalize.** Work in a group. Discuss these questions.

1. Do you consider yourself a multitasker? If so, give examples of the number and types of things that you tend to do at the same time. If not, did you make a conscious decision not to multitask, or do you just naturally avoid it? Explain your answer.

2. If you are a multitasker, do you think you are among the small percentage of people who can effectively multitask? Support your answer by giving examples from your personal life. What activities are you able to do well at the same time? What activities are you unable to do well at the same time?

3. Do you think multitasking is new, or have people always done it? Why do you think so many people multitask? Explain your answers with specific reasons and examples.

4. Have you ever had something bad or embarrassing happen to you because you were multitasking? If so, describe what happened.

Build a school in the cloud

" Schools as we know them are obsolete. **"**

BEFORE YOU WATCH

A Read the title and the information about the TED speaker. What do you think "in the cloud" means? What type of school does Mitra want to build? Discuss your ideas with a partner.

SUGATA MITRA Educational Researcher

Educational researcher Sugata Mitra's Hole-in-the-Wall experiments have shown that, without supervision or formal teaching, children can teach themselves and each other if they're motivated by curiosity and other children's interest. In 1999, Mitra and his colleagues put a hole in a wall of a very poor neighborhood in New Delhi, installed an Internet-connected PC, and left it there (with a hidden camera filming the area). What they saw was kids playing around with the computer and in the process learning how to use it and how to go online, and then teaching each other.

Sugata Mitra's idea worth spreading is that children can be capable, self-directed learners—and learn an astonishing amount—with the help of the Internet, their peers, and the encouragement of special volunteers.

B COMMUNICATE Look at the questions and check [✓] one answer for each. Then explain your answers to a partner.

1. What kind of teacher is best for you?

   _____ a teacher who knows a lot

   _____ a kind and encouraging teacher

   _____ a teacher with high expectations

2. How do you learn best?

   _____ working with other students

   _____ working alone

   _____ working with a teacher

3. What kind of material motivates you the most?

   _____ challenging material

   _____ material that interests me

   _____ material that I need to get a job

C THINK CRITICALLY Predict. Work with a partner. Discuss these questions.

1. Read the quote on the TED speaker's photo on page 134. What does *obsolete* mean? Name something that is now obsolete.

2. Based on the title of the talk, the information about the speaker, and his *idea worth spreading*, what do you think he means when he says, "Schools are obsolete"? Which of the following do you think the speaker will mention to support this position?

   _____ classroom equipment

   _____ how much time is spent in school

   _____ the teacher's role

   _____ the student's role

   _____ textbooks

   _____ how a classroom is set up (for example, the placement of the desks)

   _____ what is taught in school

VOCABULARY

D 🎧 **2.30** The sentences below will help you learn words and phrases in the edited TED Talk. Read and listen to the sentences. Choose the correct meaning of each word or phrase in bold.

1. All of the classrooms in my son's school look **identical**. The walls are painted yellow and the teacher's desk is at the front of the room.
   a. exactly the same   **b.** important   **c.** not very active

2. The economy in this part of the country is **robust**. Most people have jobs.
   a. unchanging   **b.** very interesting   **c.** working effectively

3. He thinks that schools today are **obsolete**. He thinks they should be replaced by schools that are better suited to today's world.
   a. not useful anymore   **b.** too modern   **c.** very difficult

4. All public schools must meet the performance **standards** established by the local government. For example, all children must learn to read by the end of the third grade.
   a. a building that has been inspected and found to be safe
   b. books and other materials required for learning
   c. something against which skills or ideas are measured

5. My **hypothesis** was that students could teach themselves if they had access to computers. The results of my first experiment suggest that my **hypothesis** is correct, but I need to collect more data.
   a. experiment   **b.** strong opinion   **c.** working theory

6. There are very good **pedagogical** reasons for using computers in the classroom. One of the most important is that computers motivate students to learn.
   a. related to the theory and method of teaching
   b. related to the theory of economics
   c. related to theories of science

7. Right now, children in wealthy school districts have the best teachers and resources. The government should **level the playing field** to enable poorer students to receive the same education as richer students.
   a. build better schools   **b.** make things equal   **c.** spend money on sports

8. As a result of hours of discussion among experts, a solution finally **emerged**.
   a. appeared   **b.** left   **c.** resolved

9. Children learn best when they **tap into** their own creativity. Then they learn naturally, with very little help.
   a. force open   **b.** make use of   **c.** take away

10. The **facilities** at our new school are incredible. There's a gym with a pool, several computer labs with the latest technology, and a new cafeteria.
    a. modern buildings that are designed as classroom space for university students
    b. services, including the physical area, provided by an organization
    c. the most essential people who work at an academic institution

E COMMUNICATE Use the scale below to indicate how strongly you agree or disagree with each of the statements below. Then with a partner, take turns explaining your answers. Use the words in bold in your answers.

1 = strongly disagree   2 = disagree   3 = agree   4 = strongly agree

1. _____ The **pedagogical** advantages of online learning are greater than the advantages of learning in a traditional classroom.

2. _____ The **facilities** of a school are less important than the teachers.

3. _____ The best ideas **emerge** when you work on a team, rather than alone.

4. _____ The government should **level the playing field** in society by providing free education to everyone.

5. _____ In the future, I think libraries will probably become **obsolete**.

6. _____ Television helps children **tap into** their creativity.

learnmore For about 300 years, from the 17th to the mid-20th century, Great Britain was the world's strongest power. By 1921, the British Empire controlled more than one fourth of the world's territory, including India, the East and West Indies, Canada, Australia, and parts of Africa and Egypt. After World War I, it gained even more territory in Africa and the Pacific and added territory in the Middle East.

British Empire stamps

WATCH

F ▶ **1.34 WATCH FOR MAIN IDEAS** Read the statements for each segment of the edited TED Talk. Then watch the talk and check the statement that best expresses the main point of that segment. All of the statements are true, but only one in each segment expresses the main point.

Segment 1

1. _____ The education system that we have today was designed to produce identical people who had good handwriting and could read and do arithmetic in their heads.

2. _____ Mitra believes that because of advances in technology, the education system we have today is outdated and needs to change.

3. _____ Many people say that our education system is broken, but Mitra does not agree with them.

WORDS IN THE TALK

bureaucratic administrative machine (n): a large group of government or business departments with a lot of complex rules
clerks (n): people who keep accounts or records
slum (n): an area of a city where poor people live
Victorians (pn): people living during the rule of Queen Victoria (1835-1901)

Segment 2

4. _____ Mitra started his Hole-in-the-Wall experiments because he wanted to find a way to give poor children a good education.

5. _____ The children who participated in the Hole-in-the-Wall experiments taught themselves not only how to use a computer but also some English.

6. _____ The Hole-in-the-Wall experiments were more successful than Mitra had expected.

Segment 3

7. _____ Mitra published papers on his work because he wanted to spread his ideas.

8. _____ The children in one of Mitra's Hole-in-the-Wall experiments were able to meet the same educational standards as children in an expensive private school.

9. _____ Through the Hole-in-the-Wall experiments, Mitra showed that there is a way to level the playing field for all children, rich and poor.

Segment 4

10. _____ The grannies are necessary because there are not enough teachers.

11. _____ The grannies are very important because they motivate the students to learn.

12. _____ The grannies use the Internet to communicate with children who are in trouble.

Segment 5

13. _____ Mitra's goal is a new educational system in which teachers start the learning process and then let children self-organize and learn by themselves.

14. _____ In the School in the Cloud, grannies will provide safety and encouragement and teachers will ask important questions.

15. _____ Teachers in the SOLEs (Self-Organized Learning Environments) do not teach in a traditional way.

Sugata Mitra, Professor of Educational Technology at the School of Education, Communication, and Language Sciences at Newcastle University, during the launch of *School in the Cloud* at Kalkaji Government Girls school

G ▶ **1.35** **WATCH FOR DETAILS** Watch the segment from the edited TED Talk. Put the events in order. Write *1* next to the first event that happened, *2* next to the next event, etc.

a. _____ Mitra decided to try the Hole-in-the-Wall experiment in a small village 300 miles away from New Delhi.

b. _____ Mitra returned a couple of months later and found children there playing games on the computer.

c. _____ Mitra put a computer in a hole in a wall next to his office in New Delhi.

d. _____ Mitra published many academic papers on his experiments.

e. _____ Mitra decided to challenge his hypothesis by making the learning task more difficult.

f. _____ Mitra returned eight hours later and found children browsing the Internet.

g. _____ Mitra discovered that children could learn even difficult scientific concepts if they worked together and received encouragement.

h. _____ Mitra repeated the experiment many times.

H ▶ **1.36** **EXPAND YOUR VOCABULARY** Watch the excerpts from the TED Talk. Guess the meanings of the phrases in the box.

set the stage	how on Earth	ahead of one's time
run the show	not have the foggiest idea	spare parts

I **WATCH MORE** Go to TED.com to watch the full TED Talk by Sugata Mitra.

AFTER YOU WATCH

J **THINK CRITICALLY** **Analyze and Reflect.** Reread Sugata Mitra's *idea worth spreading* on page 134 and think about what you learned in his talk. Then discuss these questions in a group.

1. What examples does Mitra give in his talk to support his idea? Was the data convincing? Explain your answer.

2. What are the advantages of Mitra's plan? What are the disadvantages? In your notebook, make a T-chart and take notes on your ideas.

3. What do you think of Mitra's plan? Would you like to attend his School in the Cloud? If you had children, would you want them to attend his school? Explain your answers.

Put It Together

A THINK CRITICALLY Synthesize. Work in a group. Read the quotes taken from the discussion in Part 1. Discuss how Sugata Mitra would respond to each quote. If you think he would disagree with a statement, what arguments might he make to change that speaker's mind?

1. *Is the Internet making us stupid, as some experts claim? And more to the point, is it making us bad readers?*

2. *I see kids who can't remember anything and don't think that's a problem! They ask me, "Why do I need to remember that? I can just look it up on the Internet." It's absurd.*

3. *. . . reading on the Internet is fun—I can read and watch videos related to what I'm learning. Also, because I'm a visual learner, videos and pictures help me learn.*

COMMUNICATE

ASSIGNMENT Participate in a Panel Discussion You will participate in a panel discussion about Sugata Mitra's School in the Cloud. Review the ideas in Parts 1 and 2 and the listening and speaking skills as you prepare.

PREPARE

PRESENTATION SKILL Show Enthusiasm for Your Topic

When you give a presentation, it is important to show that you are enthusiastic about your topic. Often, your enthusiasm will spread to the audience and make them more interested in your ideas. You can communicate your enthusiasm through tone of voice, word choice, clear stress on key words, facial expressions, and gestures.

Watch the excerpt from the TED Talk. Pay attention to how Mitra uses tone of voice, clear stress on key words, facial expressions, and body language to communicate his enthusiasm. ▶ 1.37

B Prepare your panel discussion. Your teacher will assign you to Group A or B. Group A will present the advantages of Mitra's plan, and Group B will present the disadvantages. In both groups, students will be assigned to one of the following roles. More than one student can play each role.

Role 1: the parent of a school-age teenager	**Role 3:** a 16-year-old student
Role 2: a researcher studying trends in education	**Role 4:** a high school teacher

Follow these steps as you prepare your panel presentation.

1. As a group, prepare your list of advantages or disadvantages. You will need at least as many advantages or disadvantages as there are students in your group. Consider your roles when deciding who should present each point.

2. Come up with information to support each point from step 1. Include comparisons to traditional schools.

3. Practice your panel presentation. Decide on the order of the presenters. Practice using tone, facial expressions, body language, and word choice to communicate enthusiasm for your position. Use signal words to support your position and stress key words.

PRESENT

C Read the rubric on page 182. Notice how your group's panel presentation will be evaluated. Keep these categories in mind as you present and watch your classmates' presentations.

D Participate in the panel presentation. After each group presents, there will be time for the other group to ask questions. After the panel, provide feedback using the rubric as a guide. Add notes or any other feedback you want to share.

E **THINK CRITICALLY Evaluate.** With your group, discuss the feedback you received. Discuss what your group did well and what could have made your panel discussion even stronger.

REFLECT

Reflect on what you have learned. Check [✓] your progress.

I can
- [ ] use a T-chart to take notes.
- [ ] recognize tone and identify attitudes and feelings.
- [ ] defend a position.
- [ ] stress key words.
- [ ] show enthusiasm for a presentation topic.

I understand the meanings of these words and phrases and can use them.
Circle those you know. Underline those you need to work on.

absurd	gifted	obsolete	standard
decade AWL	hypothesis AWL	on balance	tap into
emerge AWL	identical AWL	outdated	there is no doubt
extended	impact AWL	pedagogical	up-to-date
facilities AWL	level the playing field	robust	wonder

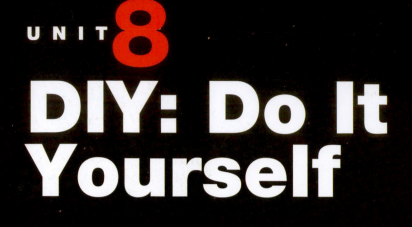

UNIT **8**
DIY: Do It Yourself

1 Read the unit title. Have you ever heard the expression "Do It Yourself" or "DIY"? What types of projects are typically "DIY"?

2 Look at the photo and read the caption. How do you think Open Source Ecology relates to the unit title? Explain.

The LifeTrac IV open-source tractor by Open Source Ecology, 2012. Open Source Ecology was founded by TED speaker Marcin Jakubowski. It is a network of farmers, engineers, architects, and supporters that uses open-source technology to allow for the construction of different industrial machines to build a civilization with modern-day comforts.

PART 1
The Psychology behind DIY

Listening
Understand Content-Rich Material

Speaking
Explain a Process

Pronunciation
Intonation in Lists

PART 2
TEDTALKS

Marcin Jakubowski
Open-sourced blueprints for civilization

Note Taking
Record Information from Lists

PUT IT TOGETHER

Communicate
Present and Explain a Process

Presentation Skill
Organize Information in a Logical Sequence

PART 1 The Psychology behind DIY

BEFORE YOU LISTEN

A COMMUNICATE Work in a small group. Discuss these questions.

1. Look at the photo. What are the people doing? How do you think they feel?

2. Why do you think some people like to do DIY projects, such as remodeling a house, rather than hiring someone to do it for them?

3. Why do you think some people like to make things for themselves—for example, knitting a sweater or building a piece of furniture—rather than buying them?

4. Do you like to make or build things yourself? If yes, what kinds of things? If not, why not?

B 🎧 2.31 THINK CRITICALLY Predict. Think about the title of the lecture and listen to the first section. In a group, make a list of questions in your notebook that you think the lecture will answer.

A husband and wife remodel an old home.

VOCABULARY

C 🎧 **2.32** Read and listen to the sentences with words from the lecture. Choose the correct meaning or explanation of each bold word.

1. The table I bought was cheap, but I had to **assemble** it myself. The instructions were terrible. It took me hours!
   - **a.** pay for
   - **b.** deliver
   - **c.** put together

2. Many business people saw the **potential** for making money with DIY products, so they started to develop products that people could make themselves.
   - **a.** certainty
   - **b.** difficulty
   - **c.** possibility

3. Despite the slow economy, the sales of our DIY projects have been very good this month. We hope to **maintain** or even increase sales next month.
   - **a.** improve a little
   - **b.** keep at the same rate
   - **c.** slow down

4. Some **consumers** buy furniture that they need to put together themselves because it's cheaper. A **consumer** is someone who _____ .
   - **a.** buys things
   - **b.** makes things
   - **c.** wants to save money

5. More and more businesses are beginning to reduce their dependence on oil because it is not a **sustainable** source of energy. Instead, they are beginning to invest in forms of energy that will always be available, such as wind and solar.
   - **a.** able to continue to exist and grow
   - **b.** acceptable to everyone
   - **c.** easy and ready to use

6. My brother likes to do projects in his free time. I've never seen him sit down and just watch television. He doesn't like to be **idle**. Someone who is **idle** doesn't _____ .
   - **a.** feel alone
   - **b.** have work to do
   - **c.** like to relax

7. The researchers are looking for people to be in their study. **Participants** have to be over the age of 21. A **participant** is someone who _____ .
   - **a.** is 22 or older
   - **b.** takes part in a research study
   - **c.** works in a research lab

8. There are two **versions** of the instructions. One is in English, and the other is in Spanish. A **version** is _____ .
   - **a.** a piece of paper with information on how to do something
   - **b.** a different type of explanation
   - **c.** a form of something that differs from other forms of the same thing

9. I bought a beautiful old table from someone on the Internet for $100. I took it to an antique dealer and he **valued** it at $1,000. Do you think I should keep it?
   - **a.** bought
   - **b.** put a price on
   - **c.** tried to sell

10. Think about the business **implications** of the results of the study. Do you think that business owners will change anything based on the research?
    - **a.** extreme difficulties
    - **b.** possible effects
    - **c.** special reasons

D COMMUNICATE Work with a partner. Read and answer these questions. Use the bold words in your answers.

1. Do you think most people **value** something more if they make it themselves or buy it? For example, think of a sweater that someone knits for a relative or a piece of furniture that you build by yourself. Explain your answer.

2. How important is it to you to have the latest **version** of a cell phone or computer program? Explain your answer.

3. What are some ways for a popular restaurant to **maintain** its popularity?

4. What is the best way for governments to encourage businesses to invest in **sustainable** energy, such as wind and solar power?

5. As a **consumer**, what are the things that influence you the most? Price? Popularity of the product? Advertising? Something else? Explain your answers with specific examples of products you have bought.

LISTEN

LISTENING SKILL   Undertstand Content-Rich Material

Lectures are often content-rich; that is, they include a lot of information. When listening to content-rich material, you might feel overwhelmed. You might get stuck on an unfamiliar word or idea and stop listening in order to figure it out. Keep listening; you often need to hear what comes *next* in order to understand what you just listened to.

🎧 **2.33** Read and listen to the example from the lecture you are going to listen to.

Now for the second study, which involved origami. Origami is the Japanese art of folding paper into different shapes, often of animals, such as birds, fish, or insects.

Notice how the speaker defines *origami* right after she mentions it.

E 🎧 **2.34** ▶ **1.38** **LISTEN FOR MAIN IDEAS** Listen to the lecture. It is divided into two segments. Each segment describes a different experiment. There will be a pause of about one minute before you hear the experiment results. Work with a partner to answer the questions and predict what the results will be. Then listen to the results and check your answers.

Experiment 1

1. What do you think most people in Group 1 did? Why do you think so?

2. What do you think most people in Group 2 did? Why do you think so?

Experiment 2

3. Which frogs do you think the participants valued more: their own or the expert-made ones? Why do you think so?

4. Which frogs do you think the people who were not involved in the experiment valued more: the participants' or the expert-made ones? Why do you think so?

F 🎧 **2.35** **LISTEN FOR DETAILS** Read the steps from the first experiment. Then listen and put them in the correct order. Write *1* next to the first step, *2* next to the second step, and so on.

a. _____ They put each participant in a separate room with a bracelet in it, and they did not let the participants take anything into the room with them.

b. _____ They gave each participant a choice. They could take the bracelet apart and put it back together, or they could do nothing.

c. _____ They told the participants to stay in the room for 15 minutes.

d. _____ The researchers divided the participants into two groups.

e. _____ They gave half of the participants instructions on how to take the bracelet apart and create a new design.

f. _____ They told the participants in Group 1 that if they took the bracelet apart, they had to put it back together in exactly the same way.

g. _____ They left the participants alone for 15 minutes.

h. _____ They gave each group a different version of the instructions.

A bracelet

G 🎧 **2.36** **LISTEN FOR DETAILS** Read the steps from the second experiment. Then listen and put them in the correct order. Write *1* next to the first step, *2* next to the second step, and so on.

a. _____ Participants valued their own origami frogs.

b. _____ Participants with no experience making origami followed instructions to make origami frogs.

c. _____ People not involved in making the frogs valued the participant-made and expert-made origami frogs.

d. _____ Participants valued expert-made origami frogs.

AFTER YOU LISTEN

H **COMMUNICATE** Work in a small group. Discuss the answers to these questions.

1. Did anything in the lecture surprise you? Explain what and why.

2. Do you agree with the hypothesis of the first experiment: Most people prefer being busy to being idle, but they need a reason to be busy? Explain your answers with specific examples from your personal experience.

3. Why do you think the participants in the second experiment valued their origami frogs so highly? Have you ever had an experience that supports or contradicts what the researchers found? Explain it to your group.

Origami frogs

THINK CRITICALLY **Interpret an Infographic.** Work in a small group. Look at the infographic and answer the questions below.

HOMEOWNER DIY: THE GROWING POPULARITY OF HOMEOWNER IMPROVEMENT PROJECTS IN THE U.S.

HOMEOWNERS AND HOME IMPROVEMENT PROJECTS, 2012

AMERICANS WHO OWNED HOMES IN 2012

35% DO NOT OWN HOMES

65% OWN HOMES

HOMEOWNERS PLANNING HOME IMPROVEMENT PROJECTS IN 2012

30% DID NOT PLAN HOME IMPROVEMENT PROJECTS

70% PLANNED HOME IMPROVEMENT PROJECTS

28% DID NOT PLAN TO DO THE WORK THEMSELVES

72% PLANNED TO DO THE WORK THEMSELVES

WHERE DO THEIR IDEAS COME FROM?

42% HOME IMPROVEMENT TV SHOWS

33% HOME IMPROVEMENT STORE DISPLAYS

32% HOME IMPROVEMENT WEB SITES

29% HOME DÉCOR MAGAZINES

Source: A-1 Equipment Rental Center

1. What is the most popular source for DIY home improvement ideas? Why do you think it is the most popular source?

2. Were you surprised at the high percentage of people who said they planned on doing their own home improvement projects? Why, or why not?

3. What percentage do you think actually completed the projects? Explain your answer.

4. If this survey were done in your country, how do you think the percentages would compare? Would they be similar? Higher? Lower? If you think there would be differences, what might some of the reasons for those differences be?

5. Do you think the information in the lecture is enough to explain the popularity of home improvement DIY in the U.S.? If not, what might some other explanations be?

SPEAKING

SPEAKING SKILL   **Explain a Process**

When you explain a process—how to do something—you can use signal words and phrases to signal steps in the process. Here are some examples:

First,   *Second,*   *Third,*   *Then,*   *Next,*   *Finally,*

After (that / 15 minutes),   *Before (that / the experiment),*

🎧 **2.37** Read and listen to the examples:

How something happened:

First, the researchers divided the participants into two groups.

Second, they put each participant in a separate room with a bracelet in it. They didn't let the participants bring anything into the room—no cell phones, books, or paper.

How to do something:

First, divide the participants into two groups.

Second, put each participant in a separate room. Don't let them bring anything into the room.

You can use the past to explain how you did something or the imperative to explain how to do something. BUT, in fact, we often use the simple present to explain how to do something.

*You **take** the…   Then you **put** the,…*

J **COLLABORATE** Work with a partner. Follow these steps.

Step 1: Look at exercise F on page 147. Add signal words where necessary. You do not need a signal word for every sentence, and sometimes more than one signal word is possible.

Step 2: Look at exercise F on page 147 again. This time, imagine that you are the head researcher for experiment 1 and you are telling your assistant how to conduct the experiment. Take turns explaining the steps of the experiment. Use signal words where necessary.

Example: *First, divide the participants into two groups.*

Step 3: Close your books. Take turns explaining the steps of the experiment to your partner. Use the imperative, the simple present, and signal words where necessary.

PRONUNCIATION SKILL   Intonation in Lists

When speakers list three or more things, they use rising intonation on all of the items in the list except for the final item, where they use either falling intonation or rising and then falling intonation.

🎧 **2.38** Read and listen to the example.

They didn't let the participants bring anything into the room—no cell phones, books, or paper.

K 🎧 **2.39** Listen and mark the items in the list with rising (↗) and/or falling (↘) arrows according to the intonation you hear. Use the sentence in the Pronunciation Skill box above as an example.

1. There are many Web sites where you can design your own products; for example, T-shirts, sneakers, jeans, or cell-phone covers.

2. DIY projects include cooking, gardening, knitting, and sewing.

3. There are DIY projects for all age groups: children, teenagers, adults, and the elderly.

4. People enjoy making origami of animals, such as birds, fish, and insects.

5. Researchers have conducted many experiments to test the effects of idleness on people's mental, emotional, and physical health.

L 🎧 **2.39** Listen again and check your markings in exercise K. Then practice reading the sentences with a partner. Check your partner's stress and intonation.

M COMMUNICATE Complete each of the sentences with your own ideas. Then say your sentences to a partner. Practice the correct stress and intonation of your lists. Use the same word form for all of the items in your list; for example, use all nouns in 1, all gerunds (-ing form) in 2, etc.

1. Some of the reasons I decided to take classes at this program are because of the _____, the _____, and the _____.

2. Some good ways to learn and remember new vocabulary are _____, _____, and _____.

3. There are a lot of things you can do to practice your English outside of class, for example, _____, _____, and _____.

Open-sourced blueprints for civilization

❝ . . . a single burned DVD is effectively a civilization starter kit. ❞

BEFORE YOU WATCH

A Read the title, the information about the TED speaker, and the key terms below. Which of the following statements do you think are true about the TED speaker? Discuss your ideas with a partner.

    a. He grew up on a farm.

    b. He has a PhD in physics.

    c. He is concerned about the environment.

    d. He studied software engineering.

MARCIN JAKUBOWSKI Farmer and Technologist

Marcin Jakubowski is the founder of Open Source Ecology, which is creating the Global Village Construction Set—the blueprints for simple construction of everything needed to start a self-sustaining village (starting cost: $10,000). At Factor e-Farm in rural Missouri, he's been successfully putting those ideas to the test.

Marcin Jakubowski's idea worth spreading is that open-source technology can enable human creativity and create more environmentally sustainable methods of production.

Key terms

open-sourced: information that is published on the Internet that others can use or adapt for free. It is available ("open") to anyone with an Internet connection.

blueprint: a design plan or technical drawing that shows you how to build something, for example, a machine or a house

self-sustaining village: a small town where everything the community needs to survive (for example, food, shelter, energy) is made right in the village

a starter kit: a starter kit is something that contains all of the material and instructions you need to start a DIY project

---

B **COMMUNICATE** Work with a partner. Discuss these questions.

1. Why would someone want to set up a self-sustaining village?

2. What kinds of blueprints do you think you would need in order to build a self-sustaining village?

3. What kind of information is the TED speaker making available? Why do you think he is doing it?

4. Look at the quote on page 152. What do you think a "civilization starter kit" might be?

C THINK CRITICALLY Predict. Work with a new partner. Think about and compare your answers from exercise A on page 153. Then discuss what you think the TED speaker is probably going to present in his talk.

VOCABULARY

D 🎧 **2.40** The sentences below will help you learn words in the TED Talk. Read and listen to the sentences and guess the meanings of the words in bold. Then write each word or phrase next to its definition on page 155.

   a. When I **set out** to do something, I am usually successful in completing it.

   b. After the earthquake, people whose houses were destroyed had to move. They started a **settlement** just outside of town, close to the river.

   c. The new machines helped increase **productivity** on the farm. They helped the farmers do their work faster and more efficiently.

   d. His ideas are **sound**. He has developed them over years of research.

   e. In some countries, the **distribution** of wealth is quite unequal. For example, one percent of the people might control 99 percent of the wealth.

   f. In today's world, there are many different **means** of communication: email, text messages, telephone, etc.

   g. You can only **transcend** your fear if you understand what you are afraid of and face it directly. By facing your fear, you can often get past it and move on.

   h. When there is a large **supply** of houses and very few buyers, house prices go down. On the other hand, when there is a **scarcity** of houses and a lot of potential buyers, housing prices rise. This is called the law of **supply** and demand.

   i. Using machines rather than human workers, factories are able to make products on a large **scale**. For example, a shoe factory might be able to produce a thousand pairs of shoes a day, while someone making shoes by hand can only work on a small **scale**, making two pairs a day.

A shoemaker works in his shop, Alexandria, Egypt.

1. _____ (phrasal v) begin an action or plan

2. _____ (n) a quantity of products

3. _____ (n) a very small or limited amount of something

4. _____ (n) a new area where a group of people has decided to live

5. _____ (n) the relationship between how many quality products and services each worker or industry can produce in a given amount of time

6. _____ (n) in a big or small way

7. _____ (n) methods or ways

8. _____ (n) spread or placement over an area

9. _____ (adj) logical; supported by evidence

10. _____ (v) overcome; go past the limitations

E **COMMUNICATE** Read the statements. Are they true or false for you? Write T for *true* or F for *false* for each statement. Then explain your answers to a partner.

1. _____ When I **set out** to do something, I sometimes get distracted and don't finish what I started.

2. _____ The **productivity** of workers in my country is high, compared to other countries.

3. _____ The **distribution** of wealth in my country is very unequal.

4. _____ One day, human beings will be able to **transcend** their differences and live in peace.

5. _____ One of the biggest problems facing humanity is the **scarcity** of water.

6. _____ I think it would be exciting to live in a small **settlement** far away from a big city.

WATCH

F ▶ **1.39** **WATCH FOR MAIN IDEAS** Watch the TED Talk. Check [✓] the three phrases that express what Jakubowski is trying to achieve. Then compare your answers with a partner's. If you did not check a statement, explain why.

1. _____ teach people how to live without modern technology

2. _____ help people live in a way that does not hurt the environment

3. _____ sell machines to the public that are easy to fix and last a long time

4. _____ teach people how to achieve high productivity in a small business environment

5. _____ help people become more self-reliant and less dependent on large industry and corporations

learnmore These days, many Americans are involved in activities to help the environment. One popular activity is to join a CSA. *CSA* stands for Community-Supported Agriculture. If you are a member of a CSA, you pay to have a local farm deliver fresh fruits and vegetables to you.

NOTE-TAKING SKILL **Record Information from Lists**

When you are taking notes, listen for the speaker's intonation as he or she lists items. If the list is long, write down as much as you can. Often, even writing one item in the list will help you understand the speaker's point. Later you may remember other items from the list and you can add them to your notes.

Read the example and look at the notes.

If we can lower the barriers to farming, building, manufacturing, then we can unleash just massive amounts of human potential.

Notes during talk: **lower barriers to farming, bldg., _____ → use more human potential**

Notes after talk: **lower barriers to farming, bldg., mfg → use more human potential**

G ▶ **1.40** **WATCH FOR DETAILS** Watch the segments from the TED Talk and take notes to answer the questions. Concentrate on writing down as many items in the lists as you can. You will see each segment two times.

Segment 1: What is Jakubowski's background?

_____

What were some of the most important machines that Jakubowski needed?

_____

Segment 2: What were the characteristics of the machines and tools he needed?

_____

Segment 3: What information has he published on his wiki?

_____

Segment 4: What are the barriers that he wants to lower?

_____

Segment 5: Who does this work help, and what does it help them to do?

_____

_____

H COMMUNICATE Work with a partner. Compare your notes from exercise G. Add items to your lists if possible.

I ▶ 1.41 Read the questions and answer choices. Use your notes from exercise G to help you choose the correct answer to each question. Then watch the segments from the TED Talk and check your answers.

Segment 1

1. How will Jakubowski's idea allow people to save money?
   a. Using his free designs and instructions, they can build their own machines.
   b. They can use his Web site to design machines that he will build for them.

Segment 2

2. What did Jakubowski discover when he tried to set up his own environmentally sustainable farming community?
   a. He was able to build his own tools and machines, but they broke too easily, they were difficult to repair, and his productivity was too low.
   b. The tools and machines he needed were too expensive to buy, broke too easily, and were too difficult or even impossible to fix.

Segment 3

3. What did Jakubowski do to solve the problem?
   a. He proved that he could achieve industrial productivity on a small scale and got people from all over the world to invest money in his project.
   b. He built tools and machines that allowed him to achieve high productivity and then made his designs available to others on the Internet.

J COMMUNICATE Work with a partner. Compare your answers from exercise I.

K ▶ 1.42 EXPAND YOUR VOCABULARY Watch the excerpts from the TED Talk. Guess the meanings of the phrases in the box.

at a fraction of the cost	be broke	show up	unleash	supply chain

WORDS IN THE TALK

the grid (n): the electrical power system managed by large utility companies
prototype (n): working model of a machine or other object used to test it before producing the final version
repository (n): a place to store objects or information where they can be easily accessed
wiki (n): a Web site that allows users to change or add things on it

A farmer driving a bulldozer

AFTER YOU WATCH

L **THINK CRITICALLY** **Evaluate.** Work with a partner. Imagine that you are starting a settlement. Which machines would you need most? Look at the descriptions of some of the machines that are included on the Open Source Ecology Web site. Then choose five of the machines.

1. *a microhouse:* a small, energy efficient, low-cost house for two people

2. *a 50kW wind turbine:* a machine that produces electricity from wind energy

3. *an open-source truck:* a vehicle used to transport large amounts of material

4. *a universal seeder:* a machine that can plant seeds for crops, such as wheat or potatoes

5. *a dairy milker:* a device that gets the milk from cows and goats

6. *a bulldozer:* a large machine that can clear land

7. *a backhoe:* a large machine that can dig large, deep holes in the ground

8. *an ironworker:* a machine that cuts steel and makes holes in it

9. *a tractor:* a large powerful machine used for construction and farm work

10. *a well-digging rig:* a machine that digs wells for water

11. *a cement mixer:* a machine that mixes the ingredients that make cement

12. *a bakery oven:* an oven used for baking bread

M **THINK CRITICALLY** **Compare.** Form a group with another pair of students. Compare and explain your choices from exercise L.

N **COMMUNICATE** Work with a partner. Discuss these questions.

1. Jakubowski mentions that participants from all over the world have traveled to his farm to help him develop the Global Village Construction Set. Would you like to visit Jakubowski's farm and meet him? Would you like to be involved in his project? Why, or why not?

2. Do you think Jakubowski will achieve his goal of completing the Global Village Construction Set? Why, or why not?

Put It Together

A **THINK CRITICALLY** **Synthesize.** Work in a small group. Consider the lecture from Part 1, *The Psychology behind DIY*, the TED Talk from Part 2, and your own experience as you discuss these questions.

1. What motivates people to do or make things themselves, rather than hiring someone else or buying something? Think of as many motivations as you can.

2. Now think about what benefits people receive from doing or making things themselves.

COMMUNICATE

ASSIGNMENT **Present and Explain a Process** You will present and explain a process to a partner. Review the ideas in Parts 1 and 2, and the listening and speaking skills as you prepare for your presentation.

PREPARE

PRESENTATION SKILL **Organize Information in a Logical Sequence**

If you organize your ideas and information well, you can say a lot in a short amount of time. Marcin Jakubowski's TED Talk is only four minutes long, yet he manages to explain a complex process. Here are some guidelines for organizing a process into a logical sequence.

- Break the process down into a series of short, individual steps. If a step is long, break it down into two or more shorter steps.

- Use simple language to describe each step.

- If you need to explain why a step is necessary, do so before you introduce the step.

- If you need to explain the result or effect of a step, do so immediately after you explain the step.

- Use signal words, such as the ones form the Speaking Skill box on page 150, to signal that you have finished one step and are moving on to the next one.

B 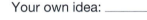 **1.43** Read the sentences from the TED Talk that explain the steps in a process. Then watch the segment and put the steps in order. Write *1* next to the first step of the process, *2* next to the second step, and so on.

a. _____ *And I found that industrial productivity can be achieved on a small scale.*

b. _____ *And now the project is beginning to grow on its own.*

c. _____ *… prototyping new machines during dedicated project visits.*

d. _____ *I found that I would have to build them (the machines) myself.*

e. _____ *Then contributors from all over the world began showing up.*

f. _____ *So I did just that.*

g. _____ *So then I published the 3D designs, schematics, instructional videos, and budgets on a wiki.*

h. _____ *And I tested them.*

i. _____ *So far, we have prototyped eight of the fifty machines.*

C Choose a process to present to a classmate. You can use one of the suggestions below, or you can think of your own idea.

How to build, make, or fix something   How to plant a garden

How to play a game   How to use a computer program or mobile application

Your own idea: _____

D Prepare for your presentation. Follow these steps.

1. Break the process down into small steps.

2. Put key words for each step on one note card. Write a signal word in front of each new step.

3. Put the steps in a logical order. Write a number on each note card.

PRESENT

E Read the rubric on page 182. Notice how your presentation will be evaluated. Keep these categories in mind as you present and watch your classmate's presentation.

F Give your presentation to a partner. After your partner finishes evaluating you, your partner presents and you assess him or her. Use the rubric as a guide. Add notes or any other feedback you want to share.

G THINK CRITICALLY Evaluate. With your partner, discuss the feedback you received. Discuss what you did well and what might make your presentation even stronger.

REFLECT

Reflect on what you have learned. Check [✓] your progress.

I can
- ☐ understand content-rich material.
- ☐ explain a process.
- ☐ use rising and falling intonation in lists.
- ☐ record information that is given in lists.
- ☐ organize information in a logical sequence.
- ☐ present and explain a process.

I understand the meanings of these words and can use them.
Circle those you know. Underline those you need to work on.

assemble AWL	maintain AWL	scale	supply
consumer AWL	means	scarcity	sustainable AWL
distribution AWL	participant AWL	set out	transcend
idle	potential AWL	settlement	value
implication AWL	productivity	sound	version AWL

Independent Student Handbook

The *Independent Student Handbook* is a resource you can use during and after this course. It provides additional support for listening, speaking, note-taking, pronunciation, presentation, and vocabulary skills.

Listening Strategies

Predicting

Speakers giving formal talks usually begin by introducing themselves and then introducing their topic. Listen carefully to the introduction of the topic, and try to anticipate what you will hear.

Strategies:

- Use visual information including titles on the board, on slides, or in a PowerPoint presentation.
- Think about what you already know about the topic.
- Ask yourself questions that you think the speaker might answer.
- Listen for specific introduction phrases.

Listening for Main Ideas

It is important to be able to tell the difference between a speaker's main ideas and supporting details. In college, professors will often test students' understanding of the main ideas more than of specific details.

Strategies:

- Listen carefully to the introduction. The main idea is often stated at the end of the introduction.
- Listen for rhetorical questions, or questions that the speaker asks and then answers. Often the answer is the statement of the main idea.
- Notice ideas that are repeated or rephrased. Repetition and rephrasing often signal main ideas (see Common Phrases for Presenting, Repeating and Rephrasing, page 165).

Listening for Details (Examples)

A speaker will often provide examples that support a main idea. A good example can help you understand and remember the main idea better.

Strategies:

- Listen for specific phrases that introduce an example (see Common Phrases for Presenting, Giving Examples, page 165).
- Notice if an example comes after a general statement from the speaker.
- If there are several examples, decide if they all support the same idea.

Listening for Details (Reasons)

Speakers often give reasons or list causes and/or effects to support their ideas.

Strategies:

- Notice nouns that might signal causes/reasons (e.g., *factors, influences, causes, reasons*) or effects/results (e.g., *effects, results, outcomes, consequences*).
- Notice verbs that might signal causes/reasons (e.g., *contribute to, affect, influence, determine, produce, result in*) or effects/results (often these are passive, e.g., *is affected by*).
- Listen for specific phrases that introduce reasons/causes and effects/results (see Common Phrases for Presenting, Giving Reasons or Causes, and Giving Results or Effects, page 164).

Understanding the Structure of the Presentation

An organized speaker will use certain expressions to alert you to the important information that will follow. Notice signal words and phrases that tell you how the presentation is organized and the relationship between main ideas.

Introduction

A good introduction includes something like a thesis statement, which identifies the topic and gives an idea of how the lecture or presentation will be organized. Here are some expressions to listen for that indicate a speaker is introducing a topic (see also Common Phrases for Presenting, Introducing a Topic, page 164):

I'll be talking about …	*My topic is …*
There are basically two groups …	*There are three reasons …*

Body

In the body of the lecture, the speaker will usually expand upon the topic. The speaker will use phrases that tell you the order of events or subtopics and their relationship to each other. Here are some expressions to listen for to help follow the body of a lecture (see also Common Phrases for Presenting, Listing or Sequencing, page 164):

The first / next / final (point) is …	*First / Next / Finally, let's look at …*
Another reason is …	*However, …*

Conclusion

In a conclusion, the speaker often summarizes what has already been said and may discuss what it means or make predictions or suggestions. Sometimes speakers ask a question in the conclusion to get the audience to think more about the topic. Here are some expressions to listen for that indicate a speaker is giving a conclusion (see also Common Phrases for Presenting, Conclusion, page 165):

In conclusion, …	*In summary, …*
As you can see …	*To review, + (restatement of main points)*

Understanding Meaning from Context

Speakers may use words that are new to you, or you may not understand exactly what they've said. In these situations, you can guess the meaning of a particular word or fill in the gaps of what you've understood by using the context or situation itself.

Strategies:

- Don't panic. You don't always understand every word of what a speaker says in your first language, either.
- Use context clues to fill in the gaps. What did you understand just before or just after the missing part? What did the speaker probably say?
- Listen for words and phrases that signal a definition or explanation (see Common Phrases for Presenting, Signaling a Definition, page 165).

Recognizing a Speaker's Bias

Speakers often have an opinion about the topic they are discussing. It's important for you to know if they are objective or subjective about the topic. Objective speakers do not express an opinion. Subjective speakers have a bias or strong feeling about the topic.

Strategies:

- Notice words like adjectives, adverbs, and modals that the speaker uses (e.g., *ideal, horribly, should, shouldn't*). These suggest that the speaker has a bias.
- Listen to the speaker's tone. Does he or she sound excited, happy, or bored?
- When presenting another point of view on the topic, is that other point of view given much less time and attention by the speaker?
- Listen for words that signal opinions (see Common Phrases for Classroom Communication, Expressing Opinions, page 166).

Common Phrases for Presenting

The chart below provides some common signal words and phrases that speakers use in the introduction, body, and conclusion of a presentation.

INTRODUCTION

Introducing a Topic	
I'm going to talk about …	*Today we're going to talk about …*
My topic is …	*So we're going to show you …*
I'm going to present …	*Now / Right / So / Well,* (pause) *let's look at …*
I plan to discuss …	*There are three groups / reasons / effects / factors …*
Let's start with …	*There are four steps in this process.*

BODY

Listing or Sequencing	Signaling Problems/Solutions
First / First of all / The first (noun) / *To start / To begin, …*	*The one problem / issue / challenge* (with) *is …*
Second / Secondly / The second / Next / Another / Also / Then / In addition, …	*The one solution / answer / response is …*
Last / The last / Finally …	
There are many / several / three types / kinds of / ways, …	

Giving Reasons or Causes	Giving Results or Effects
Because + (clause): *Because it makes me feel happy …*	*so +* (clause): *so I went to the symphony*
Because of + (noun phrase): *Because of climate change …*	*Therefore, +* (sentence): *Therefore, I went to the symphony.*
Due to + (noun phrase) …	*As a result, +* (sentence).
Since + (clause) …	*Consequently, +* (sentence).
The reason that I like hip-hop is …	*… causes +* (noun phrase)
One reason that people listen to music is …	*… leads to +* (noun phrase)
One factor is + (noun phrase) …	*… had an impact / effect on +* (noun phrase)
The main reason that…	*If … then …*

Giving Examples	**Repeating and Rephrasing**
The first example is…	*What you need to know is …*
Here's an example of what I mean …	*I'll say this again, …*
For instance, …	*So again, let me repeat …*
For example, …	*The most important point is …*
Let me give you an example …	
… such as …	
… like …	
Signaling Additional Examples or Ideas	**Signaling to Stop Taking Notes**
Not only … but	*You don't need this for the test.*
Besides …	*This information is in your books / on your handout / on the Web site.*
Not only do … but also	*You don't have to write all this down.*
Identifying a Side Track	**Returning to a Previous Topic**
This is off-topic, …	*Getting back to our previous discussion, …*
On a different subject, …	*To return to our earlier topic …*
As an aside, …	*OK, getting back on topic …*
That reminds me ….	*So to return to what we were saying, …*
Signaling a Definition	**Talking about Visuals**
Which means …	*This graph / infographic / diagram shows / explains …*
What that means is …	*The line / box / image represents …*
Or …	*The main point of this visual is …*
In other words, …	*You can see …*
Another way to say that is …	*From this we can see …*
That is …	
That is to say …	

CONCLUSION

Concluding	
Well / So, that's how I see it.	
In conclusion, …	
In summary, …	
To sum up, …	
As you can see, …	
At the end, …	
To review, + (restatement of main points)	

Common Phrases for Classroom Communication

The chart below shows some common phrases for expressing ideas and opinions in class and for interacting with your classmates during pair and group work exercises.

PHRASES FOR EXPRESSING YOURSELF

Expressing Opinions	Expressing Likes and Dislikes
I think …	*I like …*
I believe …	*I prefer …*
I'm sure …	*I love …*
In my opinion/view …	*I can't stand …*
If you ask me, …	*I hate …*
Personally, …	*I really don't like …*
To me, …	*I don't care for …*

Giving Facts	Giving Tips or Suggestions
There is evidence/proof …	Imperatives (e.g., *Try to get more sleep.*)
Experts claim/argue …	*You/We should/shouldn't …*
Studies show …	*You/We ought to …*
Researchers found …	*It's (not) a good idea to …*
The record shows …	*I suggest (that) …*
	Let's …
	How about + (noun/gerund)
	What about + (noun/gerund)
	Why don't we/you …
	You/We could …

PHRASES FOR INTERACTING WITH OTHERS

Agreeing	Disagreeing
I agree.	*I disagree.*
True.	*I'm not so sure about that.*
Good point.	*I don't know.*
Exactly.	*That's a good point, but I don't agree.*
Absolutely.	*I see what you mean, but I think that …*
I was just about to say that.	
Definitely.	
Right!	

PHRASES FOR INTERACTING WITH OTHERS

Clarifying / Checking Your Understanding

So are you saying that … ?

So what you mean is … ?

What do you mean?

How's that?

How so?

I'm not sure I understand/follow.

Do you mean … ?

I'm not sure what you mean.

Asking for Clarification/Confirming Understanding

Sorry, I didn't catch that. Could you repeat it?

I'm not sure I understand the question.

I'm not sure I understand what you mean.

Sorry, I'm not following you.

Are you saying that…?

Do you mean that…?

If I understand correctly, you're saying that …, right?

Oh, now I get it. You're talking about…, right?

Checking Others' Understanding

Does that make sense?

Do you understand?

Do you see what I mean?

Is that clear?

Are you following me?

Do you have any questions?

Asking for Opinions

What do you think?

We haven't heard from you in a while.

Do you have anything to add?

What are your thoughts?

How do you feel?

What's your opinion?

Taking Turns

Can I say something?

May I say something?

Could I add something?

Can I just say … ?

May I continue?

Can I finish what I was saying?

Would you finish what you were saying?

Did you finish your thought?

Let me finish.

Let's get back to …

Interrupting Politely

Excuse me.

Pardon me.

Forgive me for interrupting, …

I hate to interrupt, but …

Can I stop you for a second?

Asking for Repetition

Could you say that again?

I'm sorry?

I didn't catch what you said.

I'm sorry. I missed that. What did you say?

Could you repeat that, please?

Showing Interest

I see.	*Good for you.*
Really?	*Seriously?*
Um-hmm.	*No kidding!*
Wow.	*And? (Then what?)*
That's funny/amazing/incredible/awful!	

Note-Taking Strategies

Taking notes is a personalized skill. It is important to develop a note-taking system that works well for you. However, there are some common strategies that you can use to improve your note taking.

BEFORE YOU LISTEN

Focus Try to clear your mind before the speaker begins so you can pay attention. If possible, review previous notes or what you already know about the topic.

Predict If you know the topic of the talk, think about what you might hear.

LISTEN

Take Notes by Hand

Research suggests that taking notes by hand rather than on a laptop or tablet is more effective. Taking notes by hand requires you to summarize, rephrase, and synthesize the information. This helps you *encode* the information, or put it into a form that you can understand and remember.

Listen for Signal Words and Phrases

Speakers often use signal words and phrases (see page 164) to organize their ideas and indicate what they are going to talk about. Listening for signal words and phrases can help you decide what information to write down in your notes.

Today we're going to talk about three alternative methods that are ecofriendly, fast, and efficient.

Condense (Shorten) Information

- As you listen, focus on the most important ideas. The speaker will usually repeat, define, explain, and/or give examples of these ideas. Take notes on these ideas.

    Speaker: *Worldwide, people are using and wasting huge amounts of plastic. For example, Americans throw away 35 million plastic bottles a year.*

    Notes: *Waste plastic*
    Amer. 35 mil plastic bottles/year

- Don't write full sentences. Write only key words (nouns, verbs, adjectives, and adverbs), phrases, or short sentences.

    Full sentence: *The Maldives built a sea wall around the main island of Male.*

    Notes: *Built sea wall—Male*

- Leave out information that is obvious.

    Full sentence: *Van den Bercken fell in love with the music of Handel.*

    Notes: *VDB loves Handel*

- Write numbers and statistics. (*35 mil; 91%*)

- Use abbreviations (e.g., *ft., min., yr.*) and symbols (=, ≠, >, <, %, →).

- Use indenting. Write main ideas on the left side of the paper. Indent details.

    Benefits of car sharing
    Save $
    Saved $300–400/mo.

- Write details under key terms to help you remember them.

- Write the definitions of important new words from the presentation.

AFTER YOU LISTEN

- Review your notes soon after the lecture or presentation. Add any details you missed and remember.
- Clarify anything you don't understand in your notes with a classmate or teacher.
- Add or highlight main ideas. Cross out details that aren't important or necessary.
- Rewrite anything that is hard to read or understand. Rewrite your notes in an outline or other graphic organizer to organize the information more clearly (see Organizing Information, below).
- Use arrows, boxes, diagrams, or other visual cues to show relationships between ideas.

ORGANIZING INFORMATION

Sometimes it is helpful to take notes using a graphic organizer. You can use one to take notes while you are listening or to organize your notes after you listen. Here are some examples of graphic organizers:

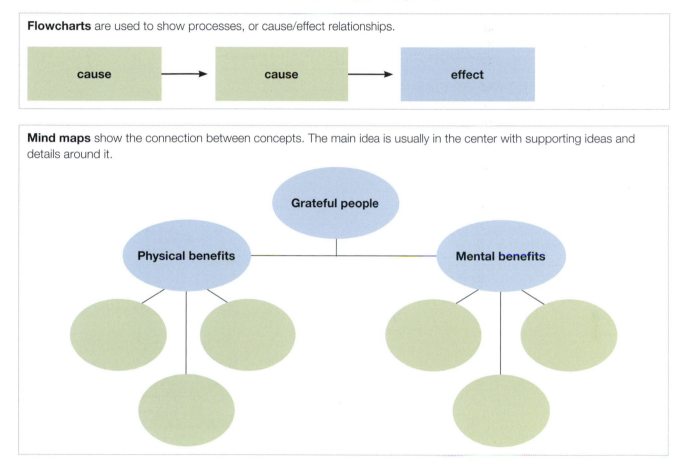

Flowcharts are used to show processes, or cause/effect relationships.

Mind maps show the connection between concepts. The main idea is usually in the center with supporting ideas and details around it.

Outlines show the relationship between main ideas and details.

To use an outline for taking notes, write the main ideas starting at the left margin of your paper. Below the main ideas, indent and write the supporting ideas and details. You may do this as you listen, or go back and rewrite your notes as an outline later.

    I.   Saving Water

         A. Why is it crucial to save water?

             1. Save money

             2. Not enough fresh water in the world

T-charts compare two topics.

Hands-On Learning	
Advantages	**Disadvantages**
1. Uses all the senses (sight, touch, etc.) 2. Encourages student participation 3. Helps memory	1. Requires many types of materials 2. May be more difficult to manage large classes 3. Requires more teacher time to prepare

Timelines show a sequence of events.

Graduated college   Got 1st job   After 2 years, got promoted   Made vice president

Venn diagrams compare and contrast two or more topics. The overlapping areas show similarities.

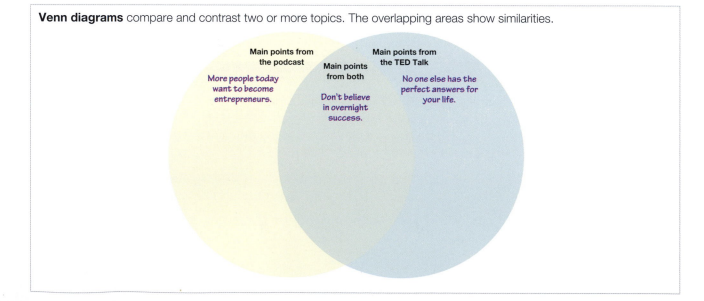

Main points from the podcast

More people today want to become entrepreneurs.

Main points from both

Don't believe in overnight success.

Main points from the TED Talk

No one else has the perfect answers for your life.

Pronunciation Strategies

When speaking English, it's important to pay attention to the pronunciation of specific sounds. It is also important to learn how to use rhythm, stress, and pausing. The charts below provide some tips about English pronunciation.

SPECIFIC SOUNDS

Vowels			Consonants		
Symbol	Key Word	Pronunciation	Symbol	Key Word	Pronunciation
/ɑ/	hot	/hɑt/	/b/	boy	/bɔɪ/
	far	/fɑr/	/d/	day	/deɪ/
/æ/	cat	/kæt/	/ʤ/	just	/ʤʌst/
/aɪ/	fine	/faɪn/	/f/	face	/feɪs/
/aʊ/	house	/haʊs/	/g/	get	/gɛt/
/ɛ/	bed	/bɛd/	/h/	hat	/hæt/
/eɪ/	name	/neɪm/	/k/	car	/kɑr/
/i/	need	/nid/	/l/	light	/laɪt/
/ɪ/	sit	/sɪt/	/m/	my	/maɪ/
/oʊ/	go	/goʊ/	/n/	nine	/naɪn/
/ʊ/	book	/bʊk/	/ŋ/	sing	/sɪŋ/
/u/	boot	/but/	/p/	pen	/pɛn/
/ɔ/	dog	/dɔg/	/r/	right	/raɪt/
	four	/fɔr/	/s/	see	/si/
/ɔɪ/	toy	/tɔɪ/	/t/	tea	/ti/
/ʌ/	cup	/kʌp/	/ʧ/	cheap	/ʧip/
/ɛr/	bird	/bɛrd/	/v/	vote	/voʊt/
/ə/	about	/ə'baʊt/	/w/	west	/wɛst/
	after	/'æftər/	/y/	yes	/yɛs/
			/z/	zoo	/zu/
			/ð/	they	/ðeɪ/
			/θ/	think	/θɪŋk/
			/ʃ/	shoe	/ʃu/
			/ʒ/	vision	/'vɪʒən/

Source: *The Newbury House Dictionary plus Grammar Reference*, Fifth Edition, National Geographic Learning/Cengage Learning, 2014.

RHYTHM

The rhythm of English involves stress and pausing.

Stress

- English words are based on syllables—units of sound that include one vowel sound.

- In every word in English, one syllable has the primary stress.

- In English, speakers group words that go together based on the meaning and context of the sentence. These groups of words are called *thought groups*. In each thought group, one word is stressed more than the others—the stress is placed on the syllable with the primary stress in this word.

- In general, new ideas and information are stressed.

Pausing

- Pauses in English can be divided into two groups: long and short pauses.

- English speakers use long pauses to mark the conclusion of a thought, items in a list, or choices given.

- Short pauses are used between thought groups to break up the ideas in sentences into smaller, more manageable chunks of information.

INTONATION

English speakers use intonation, or pitch (the rise and fall of their voice), to help express meaning. For example, speakers usually use a rising intonation at the end of *yes/no* questions, and a falling intonation at the end of *wh-* questions and statements.

Presentation Strategies

You will often have to give individual or group presentations in your class. The strategies below will help you to prepare, present, and reflect on your presentations.

PREPARE

As you prepare your presentation:

Consider Your Topic

- *Choose a topic you feel passionate about.* If you are passionate about your topic, your audience will be more interested and excited about your topic, too. Focus on one major idea that you can bring to life. The best ideas are the ones your audience wants to experience.

Consider Your Purpose

- *Have a strong beginning.* Use an effective *hook*, such as a quote, an interesting example, a rhetorical question, or a powerful image to get your audience's attention. Include one sentence that explains what you will do in your presentation and why.

- *Stay focused.* Make sure your details and examples support your main points. Avoid sidetracks or unnecessary information that takes you away from your topic.

- *Use visuals that relate to your ideas.* Drawings, photos, video clips, infographics, charts, maps, slides, and physical objects can get your audience's attention and explain ideas effectively, quickly, and clearly. For example, a photo or map of a location you mention can help your audience picture a place they have never been. Slides with only key words and phrases can help emphasize your main points. Visuals should be bright, clear, and simple.

- *Have a strong conclusion.* A strong conclusion should serve the same purpose as the strong beginning—to get your audience's attention and make them think. Good conclusions often refer back to the introduction, or beginning, of the presentation. For example, if you ask a question in the beginning, you can answer it in the conclusion. Remember to restate your main points, and add a conclusion device such as a question, a call to action, or a quote.

Consider Your Audience

- *Share a personal story.* You can also present information that will get an emotional reaction; for example, information that will make your audience feel surprised, curious, worried, or upset. This will help your audience relate to you and your topic.
- *Use familiar concepts.* Think about the people in your audience. Ask yourself these questions: Where are they from? How old are they? What is their background? What do they already know about my topic? What information do I need to explain? Use language and concepts they will understand.
- *Be authentic (be yourself!).* Write your presentation yourself. Use words that you know and are comfortable using.

Rehearse

- *Make an outline* to help you organize your ideas.
- *Write notes on notecards.* Do not write full sentences, just key words and phrases to help you remember important ideas. Mark the words you should stress and places to pause.
- *Review the pronunciation skills* in your book. Check the pronunciation of words you are uncertain about with a classmate, with a teacher, or in a dictionary. Note and practice the pronunciation of difficult words.
- *Memorize the introduction and conclusion.* Rehearse your presentation several times. Practice saying it out loud to yourself (perhaps in front of a mirror or video recorder) and in front of others.
- *Ask for feedback.* Note and revise material that doesn't flow smoothly based on feedback and on your own performance in rehearsal. If specific words or phrases are still a problem, rephrase them.

PRESENT

As you present:

- Pay attention to your pacing (how fast or slow you speak). Remember to speak slowly and clearly. Pause to allow your audience to process information.
- Speak at a volume loud enough to be heard by everyone in the audience, but not too loud. Ask the audience if your volume is OK at the beginning of your talk.
- Vary your intonation. Don't speak in the same tone throughout the talk. Your audience will be more interested if your voice rises and falls, speeds up and slows down to match the ideas you are talking about.
- Be friendly and relaxed with your audience. Remember to smile!
- Show enthusiasm for your topic. Use humor if appropriate.
- Have a relaxed body posture. Don't stand with your arms folded or look down at your notes. Use gestures when helpful to emphasize your points.
- Don't read directly from your notes. Use them to help you remember ideas.
- Don't look at or read from your visuals too much. Use them to support and illustrate your ideas.
- Use frequent eye contact with the entire audience.

REFLECT

As you reflect on your presentation:

- *Consider what you think went well* during your presentation and what areas you can improve upon.
- *Get feedback* from your classmates and teacher. How do their comments relate to your own thoughts about your presentation? Did they notice things you didn't? How can you use their feedback in your next presentation?

Vocabulary Learning Strategies

Vocabulary learning is an ongoing process. The strategies below will help you learn and remember new vocabulary words.

Guessing Meaning from Context

You can often guess the meaning of an unfamiliar word by looking at or listening to the words and sentences around it. Speakers usually know when a word is unfamiliar to the audience, or is essential to understanding the main ideas, and will often provide clues as to its meaning.

- Repetition: A speaker may use the same key word or phrase, or use another form of the same word.
- Restatement or synonym: A speaker may give a synonym to explain the meaning of a word, using phrases such as *in other words, also called,* or *..., also known as.*
- Antonyms: A speaker may define a word by explaining what it is NOT. The speaker might say *Unlike A / In contrast to A, B is ...*
- Definition: Listen for signals such as *which means* or *is defined as.* Definitions can also be signaled by a pause.
- Examples: A speaker may provide examples that can help you figure out what something is. For example, *Paris-Plage is a **recreation** area on the River Seine, in Paris, France. It has a sandy beach, a swimming pool, and areas for inline skating, playing volleyball, and other activities.*

Understanding Word Families: Stems, Prefixes, and Suffixes

Use your understanding of stems, prefixes, and suffixes to recognize unfamiliar words and to expand your vocabulary. A stem is the root part of the word, which provides the main meaning. A prefix is before the stem and usually modifies meaning (e.g., adding *re-* to a word means "again"). A suffix is after the stem and usually changes the part of speech (e.g., adding *–ation / –sion / –ion* to a verb changes it to a noun). For example, in the word *endangered*, the stem or root is *danger*, the prefix is *en–*, and the suffix is *–ed*. Words that share the same stem or root belong to the same word family (e.g., *event, eventful, uneventful, uneventfully*).

Word Stem	Meaning	Example
ann (or *enn*)	year	anniversary, millennium
chron(o)	time	chronological, synchronize
flex (or *flect*)	bend	flexible, reflection
graph	draw, write	graphics, paragraph
lab	work	labor, collaborate
mob	move	mobility, automobile
sect	cut	sector, bisect
vac	empty	vacant, evacuate

Prefix	Meaning	Example
auto-	self	automatic, autonomy
bi-	two	bilingual, bicycle
dis-	not, negation, remove	disadvantages, disappear
inter-	between	Internet, international
mis-	bad, badly, incorrectly	misunderstand, misjudge
pre-	before	prehistoric, preheat
re-	again; back	repeat; return
trans-	across, beyond	transfer, translate

Suffix	Part of Speech	Example
-able (or *-ible*)	adjective	believable, impossible
-en	verb	lengthen, strengthen
-ful	adjective	beautiful, successful
-ize	verb	modernize, summarize
-ly	adverb; adjective	carefully, happily; friendly, lonely
-ment	noun	assignment, statement
-tion (or *-sion*)	noun	education, occasion
-wards	adverb	backwards, forwards

Using a Dictionary

A dictionary is a useful tool to help you understand unfamiliar vocabulary you read or hear. Here are some helpful tips for using a dictionary:

- When you see or hear a new word, try to guess its part of speech (noun, verb, adjective, etc.) and meaning, then look it up in a dictionary.

- Some words have multiple meanings. Look up a new word in the dictionary, and try to choose the correct meaning for the context. Then see if it makes sense within the context.

- When you look up a word, look at all the definitions to see if there is a basic core meaning. This will help you understand the word when it is used in a different context. Also look at all the related words, or words in the same family. This can help you expand your vocabulary. For example, the core meaning of *structure* involves something built or put together.

> **struc·ture** /ˈstrʌktʃər/ *n.* **1** [C] a building of any kind: *A new structure is being built on the corner.* **2** [C] any architectural object of any kind: *The Eiffel Tower is a famous Parisian structure.* **3** [U] the way parts are put together or organized: *the structure of a song‖a business's structure*
> —*v.* [T] **-tured, -turing, -tures** to put together or organize parts of s.t.: *We are structuring a plan to hire new teachers.* **-adj. structural.**

Source: *The Newbury House Dictionary plus Grammar Reference*, Fifth Edition, National Geographic Learning/Cengage Learning, 2014.

Multi-Word Units

You can improve your fluency if you learn and use vocabulary as multi-word units: idioms (*mend fences*), collocations (*trial and error*), and fixed expressions (*in other words*). Some multi-word units can only be understood as a chunk—the meaning of the phrase cannot be understood from the meaning of the individual words. Keep track of multi-word units in a notebook or on notecards.

Vocabulary Notecards

You can expand your vocabulary by using vocabulary note cards. Write the word, expression, or sentence that you want to learn on one side. On the other, draw a four-square grid and write the following information in the squares: definition; translation (in your first language); sample sentence; synonyms. Choose words that are high frequency or on the academic word list. If you have looked a word up a few times, you should make a card for it.

definition:	*first language translation:*
sample sentence:	*synonyms:*

Organize the cards in review sets so you can practice them. Don't put words that are similar in spelling or meaning in the same review set, as you may get them mixed up. Go through the cards and test yourself on the meanings of the words or expressions. You can also practice with a partner.

TED Talk Summary Worksheet

Unit: _____   Video Title: _____

Speaker: _____

What information did you learn about the speaker and his or her background?

_____

_____

_____

What hook does the speaker use?

_____

Summarize the main idea in one sentence.

_____

What was the most interesting part of the talk? What would you tell a friend about it?

_____

_____

_____

How does the speaker engage the audience? (e.g., photos, infographics, other visuals, humor, gestures, personal story)

_____

How does the speaker conclude the talk? (e.g., call to action, question)

_____

What is your opinion of the talk? What words would you use to describe it?

_____

_____

What words or phrases in the talk are new to you? Write three and their definitions.

_____

_____

_____

Answers to Unit 2, Part 1, exercise K, page 30

1. Do you want to go to a horror movie at 8:00?

2. I'm nervous about the math exam.

3. Do you want to get some pizza after class?

4. I'm going to Canada with my family this summer.

5. Today is my grandmother's 70th birthday.

6. I can't play soccer. I hurt my foot.

Presentation Scoring Rubrics

Unit 1

Note: 1= lowest; 5 = highest

The presenter ...	Name _____					Name _____					Name _____					Name _____				
1. clearly introduced three main points.	1	2	3	4	5	1	2	3	4	5	1	2	3	4	5	1	2	3	4	5
2. used appropriate examples to support each main point.	1	2	3	4	5	1	2	3	4	5	1	2	3	4	5	1	2	3	4	5
3. used signals to introduce examples.	1	2	3	4	5	1	2	3	4	5	1	2	3	4	5	1	2	3	4	5
4. restated the main point after long examples.	1	2	3	4	5	1	2	3	4	5	1	2	3	4	5	1	2	3	4	5
5. used rising and falling intonation appropriately.	1	2	3	4	5	1	2	3	4	5	1	2	3	4	5	1	2	3	4	5
6. used pauses effectively.	1	2	3	4	5	1	2	3	4	5	1	2	3	4	5	1	2	3	4	5
Overall Rating	1	2	3	4	5	1	2	3	4	5	1	2	3	4	5	1	2	3	4	5
What did you like?																				
What could be improved?																				

Unit 2

Note: 1= lowest; 5 = highest

The presenters ...	Names _____					Names _____					Names _____					Names _____				
1. gave good explanations of words and terms.	1	2	3	4	5	1	2	3	4	5	1	2	3	4	5	1	2	3	4	5
2. got the audience to participate in the presentation.	1	2	3	4	5	1	2	3	4	5	1	2	3	4	5	1	2	3	4	5
3. pronounced compound words correctly.	1	2	3	4	5	1	2	3	4	5	1	2	3	4	5	1	2	3	4	5
4. I understand the meaning of the words they taught us.	1	2	3	4	5	1	2	3	4	5	1	2	3	4	5	1	2	3	4	5
Overall Rating	1	2	3	4	5	1	2	3	4	5	1	2	3	4	5	1	2	3	4	5
What did you like?																				
What could be improved?																				

Unit 3

Note: 1= lowest; 5 = highest

The presenters ...	Group _____					Group _____					Group _____					Group _____				
1. described the robot well, explaining its features and usefulness.	1	2	3	4	5	1	2	3	4	5	1	2	3	4	5	1	2	3	4	5
2. used eye contact to involve the entire audience.	1	2	3	4	5	1	2	3	4	5	1	2	3	4	5	1	2	3	4	5
3. used gestures to support the verbal message.	1	2	3	4	5	1	2	3	4	5	1	2	3	4	5	1	2	3	4	5
Overall Rating	1	2	3	4	5	1	2	3	4	5	1	2	3	4	5	1	2	3	4	5
I am/am not going to invest in your robot because… (list reasons)																				
What did you like?																				
What could be improved?																				

Unit 4

Note: 1= lowest; 5 = highest

The presenter ...	Name _____					Name _____					Name _____					Name _____				
1. repeated and rephrased important words and information.	1	2	3	4	5	1	2	3	4	5	1	2	3	4	5	1	2	3	4	5
2. talked about the important events in the life of an unusual person.	1	2	3	4	5	1	2	3	4	5	1	2	3	4	5	1	2	3	4	5
3. used appropriate signal words to show sequence of events.	1	2	3	4	5	1	2	3	4	5	1	2	3	4	5	1	2	3	4	5
4. pronounced -ed endings correctly.	1	2	3	4	5	1	2	3	4	5	1	2	3	4	5	1	2	3	4	5
Overall Rating	1	2	3	4	5	1	2	3	4	5	1	2	3	4	5	1	2	3	4	5
What did you like?																				
What could be improved?																				

Unit 5

Note: 1= lowest; 5 = highest

The presenters …	Group _____					Group _____					Group _____					Group _____				
1. explained causes and effects clearly.	1	2	3	4	5	1	2	3	4	5	1	2	3	4	5	1	2	3	4	5
2. varied their pacing to emphasize certain information.	1	2	3	4	5	1	2	3	4	5	1	2	3	4	5	1	2	3	4	5
3. grouped their words into thought groups.	1	2	3	4	5	1	2	3	4	5	1	2	3	4	5	1	2	3	4	5
4. made logical conclusions about the survey results.	1	2	3	4	5	1	2	3	4	5	1	2	3	4	5	1	2	3	4	5
Overall Rating	1	2	3	4	5	1	2	3	4	5	1	2	3	4	5	1	2	3	4	5
What did you like?																				
What could be improved?																				

Unit 6

Note: 1= lowest; 5 = highest

The group members …	Group _____					Group _____					Group _____					Group _____				
1. clarified their ideas when someone didn't understand.	1	2	3	4	5	1	2	3	4	5	1	2	3	4	5	1	2	3	4	5
2. asked questions when they didn't understand.	1	2	3	4	5	1	2	3	4	5	1	2	3	4	5	1	2	3	4	5
3. used the correct intonation when asking questions.	1	2	3	4	5	1	2	3	4	5	1	2	3	4	5	1	2	3	4	5
4. all participated actively in the discussion.	1	2	3	4	5	1	2	3	4	5	1	2	3	4	5	1	2	3	4	5
5. followed the guidelines in the Presentation Skill box.	1	2	3	4	5	1	2	3	4	5	1	2	3	4	5	1	2	3	4	5
6. performed their roles appropriately.	1	2	3	4	5	1	2	3	4	5	1	2	3	4	5	1	2	3	4	5
Overall Rating	1	2	3	4	5	1	2	3	4	5	1	2	3	4	5	1	2	3	4	5
What did you like?																				
What could be improved?																				

Unit 7

Note: 1= lowest; 5 = highest

The presenters ...	Group _____					Group _____					Group _____					Group _____				
1. supported their positions with specific information.	1	2	3	4	5	1	2	3	4	5	1	2	3	4	5	1	2	3	4	5
2. used signal words to support their positions.	1	2	3	4	5	1	2	3	4	5	1	2	3	4	5	1	2	3	4	5
3. showed enthusiasm for the topic.	1	2	3	4	5	1	2	3	4	5	1	2	3	4	5	1	2	3	4	5
4. stressed key words.	1	2	3	4	5	1	2	3	4	5	1	2	3	4	5	1	2	3	4	5
5. asked good questions.	1	2	3	4	5	1	2	3	4	5	1	2	3	4	5	1	2	3	4	5
6. answered questions well.	1	2	3	4	5	1	2	3	4	5	1	2	3	4	5	1	2	3	4	5
Overall Rating	1	2	3	4	5	1	2	3	4	5	1	2	3	4	5	1	2	3	4	5
What did you like?																				
What could be improved?																				

Unit 8

Note: 1= lowest; 5 = highest

The presenter ...	Name _____					Name _____					Name _____					Name _____				
1. broke the process down into short steps.	1	2	3	4	5	1	2	3	4	5	1	2	3	4	5	1	2	3	4	5
2. organized the information in a logical sequence.	1	2	3	4	5	1	2	3	4	5	1	2	3	4	5	1	2	3	4	5
3. used signal words to signal the steps.	1	2	3	4	5	1	2	3	4	5	1	2	3	4	5	1	2	3	4	5
4. used correct intonation in lists.	1	2	3	4	5	1	2	3	4	5	1	2	3	4	5	1	2	3	4	5
5. I learned the process my partner taught me.	1	2	3	4	5	1	2	3	4	5	1	2	3	4	5	1	2	3	4	5
Overall Rating	1	2	3	4	5	1	2	3	4	5	1	2	3	4	5	1	2	3	4	5
What did you like?																				
What could be improved?																				

Vocabulary Index

Credits

Photo credits:

Cover: © Artist Phil Hansen/Philinthecircle.com

2-3 © Karsten Moran, **4** Richard Lautens/Toronto Star/Getty Images, **6** Richard Perry/The New York Times/Redux Pictures, **9** (tl) Tischenko Irina/Shutterstock.com, (tr) Sagir/Shutterstock.com, **11** Blend Images - Jade/Brand X Pictures/Getty Images, **13** © Ryan Lash/TED, **16** Cory Richard/National Geographic Creative, **20** John Henley/Corbis/Getty Images, **22–23** © Aline Deschamps, **24** AkilinaWinner/iStock/Getty Images Plus/Getty Images, **26** Eric Kruszewski/National Geographic Creative, **27** Romeo Ranoco/Reuters, **29** Phil Schermeister/National Geographic Creative, **31** George Grall/National Geographic Creative, **32–33** © Ryan Lash/TED, **34** Ragnar Th. Sigurdsson/Age Fotostock/Getty Images, **37** Susan Seubert/National Geographic Creative, **39** Photobyte/Alamy Stock Photo, **42–43** Spencer Platt/Getty Images News/Getty Images, **44** Design pics inc/National Geographic Creative, **47** Howard Burditt/Reuters, **48** George Pickow/Hulton Archive/Getty Images, **52** © Marla Aufmuth/TED, **56** Noboru hashimoto/Corbis Historical/Getty Images, **58** Stephen J Krasemann/All Canada Photos/Getty Images, **60** Robert Clark/National Geographic Creative, **62–63** © James Mollison, **64** © Dr. Walter Schneider, **67** © Rosalie Winard, **69** Frank Sorge/Caro/Alamy Stock Photo, **71** AP Images/Naples Daily News, Brian Tietz, **72** Phonlamai Photo/Shutterstock.com, **73** © James Duncan Davidson/TED, **74** © Phil Hansen, **76** Monique Jaques/Corbis Historical/Getty Images, **81** Bettmann/Getty Images, **82–83** © Gary Chan Photography, **84** Claus Fritzmann/DieKleinert/Alamy Stock Photo, **86** Skip Brown/National Geographic Creative, **89** Hayk Shalunts/National Geographic Creative, **91** Arko Datta (India)/Reuters, **93** © Dian Lofton/TED, **95** Jim Webb/National Geographic Creative, **98** (tr) AP Images, (cr) Elliott & Fry/Stringer/Hulton Archive/Getty Images, (br) Glasshouse Images/Newscom, **100** Taylor Kennedy-Sitka Productions/National Geographic Creative, **102–103** Kenneth Garrett/National Geographic Creative, **104** David Doubilet/National Geographic Creative, **106** James Balog/Stockbyte/Getty Images, **107** David Doubilet/National Geographic Creative, **108** Jurgen Freund/Minden Pictures, **111** Thomas Pickard/Aurora Photos, **113** © Ryan Lash/TED, **114** CB2/ZOB/WENN.com/Newscom, **116–117** Riccardo Mantero/Moment Open/Getty Images, **118** Photoshot/Newscom, **120** Nur Mikhaella Ismail/Moment/Getty Images, **122–123** © Barrington Irving, **124** Robbie George/National Geographic Creative, **127** Leslie Parrott/Vault Archives/Redux, **128** Richard Nowitz/National Geographic Creative, **131** David Alan Harvey/National Geographic Creative, **133** Geber86/ E+/Getty Images, **134** © James Duncan Davidson/TED, **137** Cofiant/Alamy Stock Photo, **138** Mint/Hindustan Times/Getty Images, **142–143** © Marcin Jakubowski/Open Source Ecology, **144** Joel Sartore/National Geographic Creative, **147** Markéta Bendová/Alamy Stock Photo, **148** nunofrgr@gmail.com/Moment Open/Getty Images, **149** Millena/Shutterstock.com, **152** © James Duncan Davidson/TED, **154** Peter Adams/The Image Bank/Getty Images, **156** Thomas Barwick/Stone/Getty Images, **158** Olga Krasavina/iStock/Getty Images Plus/Getty Images, **160** Pixdeluxe/E+/Getty Images.

Listening Credits

146–148: Sources: *Idleness Aversion* and *the* **Need for Justifiable Busyness,** Christopher K. Hsee, Adelle X. Yang, and Liangyan Wang, *Psychological Science, July 2010; vol. 21, 7: pp. 926-930., first published on June 14, 2010;* http://www.hbs.edu/faculty/Publication%20Files/11-091.pdf